Mountain Bike Steve's
WILDERNESS TREKS

Mountain Bike Steve's
WILDERNESS TREKS

A Guide to
New Hampshire's
Remote Northern Territory

Steve Langella

NICOLIN FIELDS
P U B L I S H I N G

27 Dearborn Ave., Hampton, NH 03842 (603) 926-4581

The author and Nicolin Fields Publishing assume no liability for accidents, injuries, losses or damages caused directly or indirectly by people engaged in the activities described in this book. It is the responsibility of every cyclist to ride with safety and consideration.

Library of Congress Cataloging-in-Publication Data

Langella, Steve, 1953–
    Mountain bike Steve's wilderness treks : a guide to New
Hampshire's remote northern territory / Steve Langella. -- 1st ed.
        p.   cm.
    ISBN 0-9637077-1-X (pbk. : alk. paper)
    1. All terrain cycling--New Hampshire--Guidebooks. 2. New
Hampshire--Guidebooks. I. Title.
GV1045.5.N4L35 1996
796.6'4'09742--dc20
                                                95-46914
                                                CIP

Cover design by Bob Jolin, © 1996 Nicolin Fields Publishing
Maps by R.P. Hale, © 1996 Nicolin Fields Publishing
Illustrations by Lynne C. Joseph and Dona M. Barton, © 1996 Nicolin Fields
        Publishing
Cover photo by Janet D. Langella, © 1996 Nicolin Fields Publishing
Poem by Peter C. Langella, © 1996 Nicolin Fields Publishing

First Edition/First Printing

ACKNOWLEDGMENTS

Without the following people, this book would never have been a possibility. A special thanks.

To: Peter P. Langella, my deceased father who told me just one time—but that was enough.

To: Wes McNair, a great poet, friend and professor who continues to inspire, teach and advise me.

To: John Harrigan, a great publisher, friend and outdoorsman who helped me when I needed it most.

To: Gary Bedell, a great entrepreneur, friend and weightlifter who helped me learn the region, and who encouraged and believed in me, especially when I became weak.

To: Peter C. Langella, a great brother, friend and writer whose loyalty can't be matched.

Thanks:
To: Dot Bedell for all the free meals.
To: Gary Bedell, Jr. for the first bargain. (20 dollar cabin)
To: Lynne Joseph and Dona Barton for the quality art work.
To: George Porter for keeping my one-speed mechanically sound.
To: Linda Chestney for being a perfectionist.

Is a Wheel a Wheel When It Does Not Spin?

by Peter C. Langella

Only two wheels move you:
the steel-winged spirit, driven by blood,
the sun-rimmed earth, ominous, frail:

wheels you balance,
wheels you tread,
with which you glide
or struggle
through air thick and thin,
in dark light and bright shadow,
through old wonders and new breaths.

Is there ever a day which truly ends?

So, behind you, circling,
mountains rise and rise still,

while you descend, reborn,
to rest, to dream,
and so, discover
the star-fading heights of morning.

I dedicate this book to my family, especially my son Tony, and my daughter Kristi, for granting me their unconditional love. But most of all, I dedicate it to my childhood sweetheart and wife, Janet, for always making the effort to see through the cracks of my contentious personality and for always offering her friendship.

TABLE OF CONTENTS

The map on the opposite page is an overview of the 19 rides included in the book. See Chapter 4 for route notes and detailed maps.

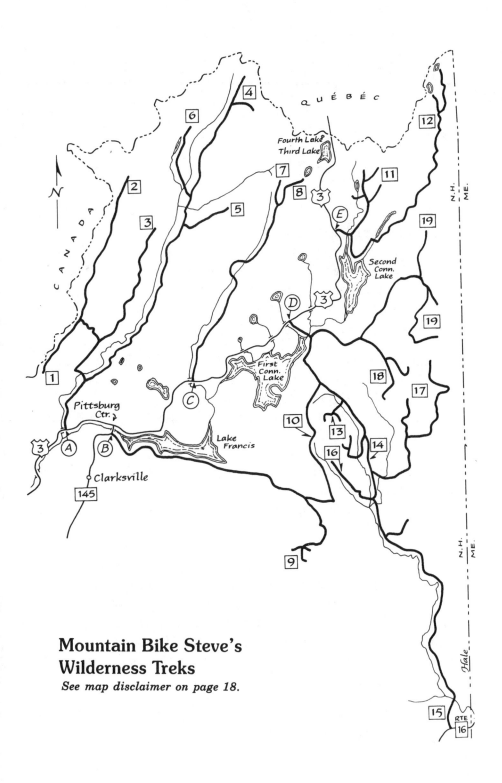

Mountain Bike Steve's
Wilderness Treks
See map disclaimer on page 18.

PREFACE

The vast majority of territory presented in this book is held by the forest industry. Champion International Corporation is the largest landowner in the region but others such as Boise Cascade Corporation, and Perry Stream Land and Timber each have considerable landshares. South of Pittsburg are a couple of large granted tracts. I'll get back to this but first let me tell you the story behind this book.

Ten years ago I seriously injured my shoulder in a workplace accident. For me, it was a tragedy because up to then I felt physically invincible. Operations were performed but the pain continued while I struggled with the notion of being limited for the first time in my life.

The first thing that went was my ability to throw. As a baseball and football coach it hurt because I could no longer coach or practice with my son. It was during a period in his life when he really needed me, too. That hurt! Recovery was erratic and much like a roller coaster as many great doctors seemed befuddled over my condition. The job went next, due to my inability to perform the required lifting. To top things off, the 81-year-old doctor who performed the surgeries as well as those of hundreds of professional athletes, including Bobby Orr, directed two unforgettable statements my way. First he said I'd never lift weights again, and second, he told me that in 10 years I'd look back at this injury and call it a blessing.

Well, it's been 10 years. I'm still in pain but am here to profess that he was right on one count and wrong on the other. My life is better because the accident weakened me physically while strengthening me mentally. This prompted me to change my ways. My life is also better because I searched endlessly to find workouts that would enable me to continue lifting weights—and have. Finally, and most importantly, my life is better because in my quest to escape discomfort I stumbled over a bike that would eventually pick me up and carry me to a world where pain had no bearing. That world—is wilderness.

After pedaling for a short time I suddenly noticed that riding provided me with relief. The pain would go away for awhile but always returned. Soon I began to pedal more and more.

It wasn't long before that extraordinary feeling of adventure which had enriched my childhood, bred new life in me—three decades later. Systematically I pedaled my single speed away from society in a quest to solve the riddle. Deeper and deeper into the solace of backcountry New England I went as my purpose became clearer. I had to find my new identity.

Each journey would be full of discovery. Hidden lands and hidden thoughts unfolded as steadily as the wheels churned. Season after season I continued. Then one day in August 1994, a forester from Champion Lumber Company approached me advising about the dangers of mountain biking on Champion property and regrettably stated that mountain bikes were not presently allowed on their lands. He went on to say that the restrictive policy was being reviewed but until a definitive change occurred, it would hold. My response was assertive.

I asked the forester how many miles he had traveled on a mountain bike. He said, "None." I went on to tell him that I had pedaled 10,000 miles in isolated country and knew well the dangers prevalent to the activity. I told him that never once had I seen a sign restricting mountain bikes, and that bikes were much less intrusive than foot travelers, autos, trucks, guns, fishing poles or snowmobiles which were all allowed on their land. I went on to say that in seven years of biking I've never had so much as a close call with a logging truck because their noise makes it quite easy to pull over into the brush and give them the right of way. In fact, I said in most instances, truckers never knew I was there. Still he persisted but advised me to write a letter to him explaining my point of view.

I did that after explaining my plans to write this book. During late winter or early spring a Champion Executive in Maine was contacted and asked about the company's mountain bike policy. He was quick to explain that in Maine mountain bikes were acceptable as long as safety issues were adhered to. He also said he had no objections to a book being written about mountain biking on Champion land as long as safety was paramount. I was thrilled, committed myself to a book contract, and set out to finalize this book.

After tons of writing and editing, my last task was to map the intended routes. Believe it or not, on the very last day of mapping (June 1995) in Pittsburg, NH, I was approached by a different Champion forester who carried the same dark message that the previous forester had given a year ago. Perplexed and aggravated, I stood in hordes of biting insects for over half an hour to plead my case right there in the woods. The forester was surprised when I told him I had permission from a Champion executive and that the same executive had no problems with mountain bikes. He was polite and agreed himself that he would love to be biking in this same area but had to follow his company's policy. We parted with his assurance to pass on my concerns and to help resolve the issue.

Since then I've spent many hours corresponding with Champion executives in hopes of having a final land-use policy for mountain bikes before printing begins. At present, I don't. Boise Cascade's land and land tracts south of Pittsburg already have an open policy for mountain biking. And ironically, Champion lands in Maine are open, too. I know, it doesn't make sense.

My choices are simple. I can terminate or delay this publication until all final policies are implemented, or go ahead with the project so that you can begin to enjoy remote mountain biking. Because I am a risk taker and an adventurer, and because I am a positive individualist and stubborn as hell, and a person who never quits—I've decided to go forward. Lastly, I'll tell you that Champion has promised me that a firm decision will be forthcoming in a reasonable time frame. I believe they will open up their lands to us. Yet to be perfectly up front, the resulting possibilities could range from no restrictions to their present restrictive policy.

In any case, my book is a valuable resource because it describes in detail how to ride your bike in the wilderness—and survive it. Remember, most private, remote lands in New England are open for your biking enjoyment. So even if Champion restricts their properties, you can use this book as a reference to ride where property owners are more accommodating. Minus the maps, of course. **In addition, my own maps are considered by some who live in the region to be the best available. If you're a hunter, hiker, bird watcher, angler, snowmobiler or boater, you can all use them to better enjoy your activity and life.**

I want you to know that trying to open the remote North Country for your biking pleasure has nearly killed me, and I'm not speaking figuratively. Yet, I'm really just an ordinary guy who's worked his butt off to bring up a family and stay above water. Anyone who knows me will attest to it.

That's why I can't put my family in jeopardy by going without the following disclaimers even though I hate to taint this book with them. Don't panic over them because the truth is, I've done the very best job I can for you and I started with no maps at all.

Finally, if things turn out unfavorably you can always call or write Champion International and implore them to reconsider their policy. I'll leave you the address of Champion's corporate office for the Northeast Division. Ask for the operation's manager. Be assertive!

Champion International Corporation Headquarters
River Road
Bucksport, Maine 04416
207-469-1700

If all else fails, contact me. I'll tell you about other great runs in Maine and New Hampshire. (Address is in back of book.)

Disclaimer:
The maps presented in this book are not drawn to scale and were prepared from information compiled while on pedal bike in 1994/1995. Mileages, roads, trails, geographical landmarks, boundary lines, improvements and monuments are roughly represented by the author who does not warrant their accuracy and completeness. Maps are intended to be a rough guide for navigational use in biking and do not imply landowners' permission. Private property and landowner restrictions must be respected. Be aware that the forest industry is actively building new roads while others systematically become overgrown and unnavigable. Land features change in a working forest as do land-use policies.

Disclaimer:
The author is not responsible for any decisions that recreational users make regarding their activities in the regions presented in this book or anywhere else.

At Stub Hill I searched for that elusive 25-pound moose rack. I didn't find the rack, but I did happen across this 25 pounds of pure quartz to add to my rock collection. After nine miles, it felt like 250!

ABOUT THE AUTHOR

Hi, I'm Steve Langella. Some people know me as Mountain Bike Steve.

It all begins in Portland, Maine in the '50s. A Great Dane, teeth bared, is breathing on my face. I'm standing inside the screen door peering out and feeling great anxiety. Nervously I watch the dog and wait. If only I can make it to the fence...

In a flash of instinct, I fling the door open and fly down the steps. I hop over the fence and sprint up the street. As I bolt, curiosity tempts me to look back. The dog sees my face and senses my terror. He quickly closes the gap between us and as he lunges for my leg, the paper boy yells, "Grey!" The dog retreats, docilely following the boy down the street, leaving me clinging to the nearest maple.

This incident shaped part of the foundation of what later became Mountain Bike Steve. Let me explain. Remember the days before leash laws? I remember them well because I lived my life in fear of stray dogs. Which made me consider how I could best avoid these roaming beasts. One summer day I glanced down the street—and saw my salvation—a blue, 24-inch, fat-tired girl's bike. The thought took root.

Beating the Bully

Another event which shaped who I am and how I became Mountain Bike Steve, began in a bully's yard at the end of Maplewood Avenue late one afternoon on a sultry Maine summer day.

The kid is a little older than me. Along with some other neighborhood kids, I watch him practice riding back and forth on the lawn. He circles around the yard again and turns my way. "Hey shrimp—you want to give it a try?" He finds that strangely humorous and laughs with his buddies. I don't hesitate. He drops the bike to the ground and I climb awkwardly onto the pedals, because I can't reach them if I sit on the seat.

Each time I get the bike rolling, he runs over and shoves me off as his cohorts break into gales of laughter. He continues this behavior until I'm crying and my knees and arms are bleeding. Yet every time I climb back on, I progress farther and wobble less. Soon the bully throws me from the bike. But I'm not quitting. I am determined to accomplish this. All the while, the bully is more and more exasperated by my success.

An older kid who was watching from across the street enters the picture. He waits until the bully is about to knock me down again and steps in, holding the bully back.

Meanwhile, I stay up for five trips around the yard before crashing. The older guy strides over, picks me up in front of the other kids and proclaims that I am the best rider of them all. Adding, "Go home, kid, and ask your Dad for a new bike. You deserve it."

Then he turns to the others and snaps, "If I catch any one of you touching that guy again, I'll personally pound you!"

I was four or five then. Dogs in packs who roamed the neighborhood taught me to deal with fear early in life. A new bike—a 20-inch red model—gave me a new sense of freedom. I spent the better part of each day pedaling. Soon dogs left me alone unless they felt like running a marathon.

Indy-500 Portland Style

This next story still causes me to chuckle. Let's go back to Portland during the same decade. Remember the homemade, two-by-four axled vehicles that kids put together? They were constructed from old lawn mower wheels with plywood bodies and clothesline steering loops.

My older brothers, ages 11 and 12, gather all the punks six years old in the neighborhood, including me. The "older boys" are obsessed with buggy racing. The little guys are the drivers. The older guys use broom sticks or poles to push the buggies. It is the Portland-style of the Indy 500. They line us up on the street five or six wide and use the poles to push us around the block at high speeds.

Some of the buggies have no clothesline steering. Rather, it's "legs on the axles." Because we're short, we're stretched out and our heads barely touch the backrest. We lie flat on our backs with necks straining to see the road.

"Gentlemen, start your engines!" someone yells. And we're off—six buggies tearing down the street with 6-year-old drivers and 12-year-old "managers" using poles. Drivers are all over the place especially the inexperienced ones. Buggies are flying into driveways, across lawns, hitting trees and fences. But the pushers know what they're doing.

They entice us with candy and soda. In fact, if you can stay on the road, they actually have fist fights over who drives for whom. In the past, I've crashed my share, but now I've become quite the commodity. All the guys are bargaining for me on race day. For decent drivers, it's sweet-tooth day. Very few of us go home and state honestly the source of our cuts and bruises—especially me. I love the thrill of control and am not about to let my mother put a stop to it.

Trap Door Terror

We left Portland, Maine, when I was six, already my second move. My father was in sales and was transferred often. The next stop was White River Junction, Vermont.

My parents, two sisters, five brothers and I moved into a giant, old house. Strangely, there was a banana tree in our yard. It never produced. The building was old and scary. My room had a trap door that opened into a creaky staircase leading to a vacant hallway that connected our apartment to the one next door.

One night the lady who lives next to us runs over to our house. She's crying hysterically. "My husband's playing with knives. He's sticking them in the kitchen table." My mother quickly sends us away, but I hear enough. Her apartment is exactly where my trap door leads.

During the same week, my grandmother, at our request, brings my sister and me to see *The Pit and The Pendulum*. The film has trap doors galore with each one leading to wicked frightening torture chambers. The movie ends as my nightmares begin. To compensate, I bang my head on the pillow to make the bed squeak—then I can forget the noises coming from the attached staircase and go to sleep.

By then I had been biting my fingernails for years and I was only seven years old. But good things happened at White River, too. One of them was the beginning of my weight lifting. Another was the beginning of my scrounging and adventuring. Let's start with weight lifting.

I Can Do That!

My father buys my older brother a weight set so he can increase his strength to play football. That night my brother has a bunch of friends over. When I hear grunts and groans coming from the laundry room, I sneak down to see what's going on. When I peek through the crack in the door, it looks like four Steve Reeves (Hercules) pumping iron.

I am impressed by their physiques and know immediately it's for me. The next day when the coast is clear, I'm in the laundry room heaving the empty bar over my head. When I get the bar above my head, I don't know how to bring it back down without dropping it on the floor or on me. Consequently, I'm straining, while my arms and knees commence a wicked shakin'. Fortunately my brother hears me yelling, darts in, and snatches it from my hands. That is my first military press—at eight years old. I've not stopped lifting since.

Treasure Collector

Now let me tell you how I became a "scrounge." As a kid, I roamed the neighborhood picking up everything and anything that interested me. Most of the time I scouted out rocks, and especially metal objects.

I systematically walk the streets looking for junk or bottles. The junk I keep in shoe boxes, piles of them. We have plenty of boxes with eight kids (eventually nine) in the family. The bottles I cash in at the store for two cents each and with the money I buy two-for-a-penny mint juleps.

A True "Greaser"

Next door to our house is St. Johnsbury Trucking Company. After they close on Saturdays, I slip over and crawl under the fifth wheel of the tractor trailers and scrape off globs of grease. I have cans full of it. The mechanics must wonder what the hell is going on. They gob it on Friday and when they return Monday, it's gone.

I treasure my junk. Occasionally one of my brothers or sisters touches my stuff when I'm gone. This sets me on a rampage until I get whatever is missing, back.

I have gold gears from a broken alarm clock. I consider them my primo collector's pieces. I believe they are pure gold. That's why I freak out when anyone gets near them without asking.

My parents don't give us kids much of an allowance. So for my brothers or sisters birthdays, I open my shoe boxes and give away my special treasures as presents. It is tough parting with heavy, metal washers because in my pocket they seem like money.

But the spirit of giving makes it worthwhile. I always feel richer afterward.

Hole in my Soul

It wasn't long before I was gathering my stash for the next move. The third in six years. In 1961 we moved to North Swanzey, New Hampshire. We moved into a nice house—one with no trap doors or spooky staircases. It was on a dead-end road with a half dozen other homes. But what made it special was the woods. My experience with the wilderness began while we lived there.

The back yard is big enough to play hide-and-seek without ever being found. We aren't supposed to venture into the woods too far, but when Ma is busy with the smaller ones, I hop the fence and begin my adventure. My first encounters in nature occur down a valley and across a stream, where the sounds of quiet and scent of evergreen entice me. I'm hooked.

Leaving behind my friends in Portland and White River begins to bother me. I feel lonely and empty thinking about them. It is hard to think I will never see them again. Missing my friends digs a hole in my soul, a hole the forest and nature begins to fill.

Making friends in North Swanzey is difficult. Being the new kid on the block is tough. As a short guy in a tall world, I'm not readily accepted. Sadly, I begin to fight. It's my way of handling rejection.

I learned early in life about close friendships. I had experienced two. Both these guys were my buddies for better or worse. Those were great days when loyalty meant something and you cared about each other's feelings. But it didn't happen in Swanzey. Instead, I found a lot of lonely time on my hands. And so, when not exploring the woods, I was riding my bike.

A New Challenge

In North Swanzey a big L-shaped hill connects a busy road on one end, with our street on the other end. Local kids race down and try to make it to the top without getting off their bikes. They don't graciously accept me, a newcomer, racing past, pedaling to the top and waiting for them to walk their bikes up.

On one particularly sunny day, with the wind behind me, I fly down and try to make the L-turn without braking. Then the challenge is reversed. The quest is to climb without rest. Feeding my appetite for challenge, I do the hill 20 times without getting off my bike. Glory is the best "nutrition" you can get. Sometimes in life the hills keep you going. You learn to persevere through life's challenges.

In less than a year our family moved again. The next stop was Waterville, Maine. We lived on North Street in a nice house in a residential area. I liked it. The place greatly influenced me. I was nine or 10 years old and quickly fell in love with sports, soapbox buggies and railroad tracks.

Gaining Respect

My father was a champion Navy boxer in WWII, so we always have gloves in the house. My oldest brother is sparring with Dad in the driveway. They are pounding each other in what looks like serious stuff, but isn't. But to me, it's *very* real. I scream for them to stop. Dad, distracted, looks in my direction. Bang! He takes a right cross in the face. Though his nose is bleeding, he never says one word to me. I am grateful.

School and neighborhood relationships improved in Maine. I excelled in the classroom and on the playground. Because I lifted weights and boxed with my brothers in the cellar, I became stronger and tougher than anyone my size or age—even some of the bigger guys. This was important because I had always been the shortest kid on the block. Then when someone reminded me of my stature, I would let them know back. I didn't enjoy fighting. I did it to gain their respect.

Suicide Hill

One summer my younger brother wins a real soapbox derby buggy in Waterville, Maine. It has official derby wheels and can roll uphill. There is nothing faster in town. Consequently, I want to ride in it all the time. But I don't own it, so have to ask permission.

One afternoon all the guys gather at Suicide Hill with their low-class buggies. The week before, a kid with a real box derby buggy like my brother's, was badly injured in a crash. The grade is okay for regular buggies with lawn mower wheels that don't roll well, but terrifyingly fast for buggies with derby wheels. Excessive speed spells danger. That's why my mother restricts me from riding on Suicide Hill.

Today a bunch of us boys gets together to play a game of "Dare." Soon it's my turn. They dare me to ride down the steep hill starting from the highest point. I think I can handle it, so when they taunt me, I take the challenge. I line up my buggy in the middle of the road, turn up my courage and I'm off.

I'm flying down Suicide Hill. Halfway down, I watch in horror as a tractor trailer backs out of a dock directly in my path. Surely the end is near. I'm flying down the hill too fast to eject.

Nine Minus One

Suddenly a thought flashes through my mind. What if I stay the course? I will! I streak right under the trailer and out the other side! There goes the first of my nine lives, and it makes me a hero on the streets.

That event was the last memory I recall about buggy riding. I think the railroad took its place.

Down the street and into the woods a short distance were the railroad tracks. Immediately after we moved, the noise from the trains began calling my name. But the older kids told us 10 year olds to stay away from there. They warned us that quicksand was everywhere. I believed it—enough to crawl on my stomach while feeling my way as if I were negotiating a mine field. One day I finally said "the hell with it" and sprinted full speed to the tracks.

When I arrive, I am instantly infatuated—and rich! Two-cent and five-cent bottles are scattered everywhere. But what hooks me is the isolation. Even though the town surrounds me, the area is quiet. I walk the tracks and notice numerous animals scooting around. Also, there is this trestle bridge...

Freight-Hopping Kid

Many a day I waited by the bridge and watched trains pass. I began to fantasize about how easy it would be to jump on for a ride. The thought haunted me. Then one morning when I heard the whistle, I bolted from the house in time to grab hold of the box car ladder. A minute later I jumped off just before the trestle. I felt like a true bum. What a high! The problem was I couldn't stop doing it—until one late afternoon when I cashed in the second of my nine lives.

I lie on my stomach a few feet into the woods, and as the train roars past, I chase it down. Today I'm sprinting toward the train, but just as I get close to the ladder, a real bum lying on the side of the tracks, startles me. I jump back and fall so close to the wheel that the noise still rings in my ear. This is my last freight-hopping adventure.

The trestle had more stories, too. My brother and I would fish off the trestle. We would catch dozens of sunfish on an average day. And it was there that we first tried out my father's Camel's.

An Explosive Experience

I will never forget the time I did a favor for an older kid. I follow the old guys around. They allow this because my big brothers don't mind and no one wants to challenge them. Black leather jackets and butts rolled in white T-shirts are in. Anyway, the favor the kid asks me is insignificant—going to the store for him. Usually I get a nickel for this task, but this time he handles the payment differently. He gives me a fingernail polish bottle—full of gun powder. The other kids often tease me because I always carry matches. The older boy tells me not to light it while the powder is in the bottle. In no time I dump the gray powder in a pile on the sidewalk and light it. It's my first, and hopefully last, observance of a mushroom cloud.

Knowing a person's childhood experiences often offers insights into how people deal with life as an adult.

Life Moves On...

John F. Kennedy was shot just before we packed for Manchester, New Hampshire. And this new move was...but you've had enough stories. This section is not intended to be an autobiography. However it is intended to help you better understand who I am. Mountain Bike Steve is who he is because of the events and experiences he's lived.

Here's who I am today. I'm a family man. I'm a teacher in the state reform school. I'm a veteran. I'm self-educated and formally educated. I'm an ordinary man. I'm a believer in choices rather than excuses. I'm a positive-attitude person. I have energy. I'm young at heart.

If I Could do it Over Again

I would relive my life exactly the same—including dogs chasing me, trap doors, nightmares, buggy rides and all the rest of my foolishness—coupled with some hard-earned successes. Wait a minute, maybe I'd cut out the dogs chasing me...? Whaaahoooo!

INTRODUCTION

If you have flipped through this book you've probably recognized that it's different. Don't worry, that's the plan. I'm Mountain Bike Steve, and by all mountain bike standards, I'm different too. Yet as you read on, you'll realize that different can be enjoyable and valuable. Here's why I'm writing.

Pedal Softly

Mountain biking is marketed by some companies in a questionable way. The activity is quickly gravitating toward speed riding, jumping, racing, skidding and generally unproductive horseplay. Many magazines and books feature pictures that inappropriately display mountain bikers competing through the woods or flying off the ground above downed trees, boulders, etc. Subsequently, many readers perceive that recklessness is normal biking. Unfortunately thrill seekers of this type are often forced into an early retirement because of injuries.

This form of mountain biking is dangerous to animals and their ecological habitats. Creatures should be able to go about their normal routine. Bikers performing foolish chicanery should be doing it under the Big Top, not under the trees. Such activity can only motivate landowners and the government to restrict mountain bike access in wilderness areas. Therefore, this book frowns on the clown and promotes a reasonable, environmental approach to mountain biking.

Mountain Biking Fosters Independence

I have pedaled my one-speed mountain bike alone for thousands of miles in isolated territory. These adventures parallel my experiences from everyday life. In other words, life and mountain biking both present adversities to overcome. There are good times, bad times, hot spells, cold spells, challenges, temptations and decisions. You encounter risk, fear, excitement and glory. Sometimes you plan. Sometimes you wing it, but always you keep going. You deal with uncertainty, weakness, insecurity, strength and confidence. While mountain biking, panic and despair occasionally surfaces—just as they do in life. Finally, and most importantly, there is bliss.

Remote mountain biking improves character and revitalizes your spirit. The adventures strengthen your resolve and broaden your mind. They enhance your thinking and compel you toward inner convictions. Yet mountain biking has its dangers, even after you employ all the measures necessary to make your ride safe.

There is always a chance you may lose control of your bike while traveling over and through the many hindrances inherent to off-tar riding. You could make bad decisions by simply biting off more than you can chew or because you're inexperienced and unprepared. Biking can be fatal. However, if you use sound judgment, you'll find wilderness mountain biking can be enjoyable, invigorating and inspiring. It's also good exercise.

Remote mountain biking is an activity that can promote a balanced and stable life-style. At the same time, it can foster independent thinking.

Mountain Bike Smarts

In this book I share my knowledge—everything I know—about wilderness riding. But bear in mind I am just an ordinary guy that usually rides a one-speed mountain bike and does not profess to be an expert.

What I do know is how to travel the logging roads and snowmobile trails of remote New Hampshire and Maine. I've been doing it for eight years without injury or serious breakdown. My off-tar trips average 50+ miles per day—totaling over 1,500 miles per season. And well over 10,000 miles cumulatively.

I merely want to share my experiences, philosophies and hard-earned biking wisdom as a wilderness adventurer—so that you can benefit from it. Very few serious off-road mountain bikers ride north of Route 2 in New Hampshire. It's probably because people think no maps exist for the areas. Some believe that they are restricted from riding there. Others fear the remoteness and wildlife. Some riders may be convinced that better riding exists in the southern tier or the White Mountain National Forest region. While there's some truth to all of these statements, it's my opinion that wilderness riding is the missing link to a mountain biker's itinerary. Come along and let me prove it.

BEFORE YOU START

Do You Have What It Takes?

The person best able to bike 30-plus miles per day in wilderness areas:

◆ Should be able to physically and mentally tax their system without fear of injury.

◆ Should know their physical and mental limits.

◆ Should be able to rise at daybreak, expend a great deal of energy for long periods with little rest, and be prepared to cope with adversity (i.e., miles of upgrades, bad weather).

◆ Should be able to think soundly under stressful conditions (i.e., breathing heavily because of amount of energy expended, losing your way).

◆ Should have a sturdy, well-balanced musculature, good vision, coordination and no medical problems.

◆ Should have great stamina—and be able to exercise cardiovascularly for hours with little rest.

◆ Should possess a high degree of initiative, self-determination, self-sufficiency and discipline.

◆ Should enjoy a challenge, accept risk of bodily injury and have excellent recuperative abilities.

◆ Should be fully comfortable and willing to venture into unknown terrain knowing there are no emergency services available.

◈ Should be able to push their bike when unable to pedal, on steep upgrades and long, steady climbs.

◈ Should be prepared to abandon their bike when necessary (mechanical problems that can't be fixed on-the-spot) and walk possibly 20 miles or more to get out of the woods.

◈ Should realize that there is a risk of dying from the elements (weather) or from bodily breakdowns due to stress.

◈ Should be aware that only crude, inaccurate maps are available for wilderness biking in the areas specific to this book.

If some of these requirements seem redundant—it's for a reason. I want you to consider these factors carefully. My experiences prove that every one is relevant. But don't be frightened off.

If you welcome a challenge with risk involved, this book is for you. If you are bold, tenacious, determined, steady, undaunted and daring, then you will identify with this book. Finally, if you are an explorer who thirsts after adventure, then this book will help you fill that need.

ABOUT THE BOOK

This book offers advice on how to prepare for wilderness rides, suggests what gear to bring with you and provides route notes and maps to show you the way. It also contains a collection of episodes called "Adventures and Thoughts with Mountain Bike Steve," that chronicle some of my experiences. Several of these stories were picked up by newspapers and ran as a series.

The stories are about remote bike rides that I, as Mountain Bike Steve, wrote for reader's enjoyment and also to explain what really happens on wilderness treks.

You can expect more from this work than just wilderness mountain biking. My goal is to offer you a prescription for harmoniously living in the present while helping you overcome adversity. And lastly, I want to share with you the insights I've gained from blending with the wilderness. I hope you enjoy it.

Chapter 1

Planning Your Ride

Preparing for Wilderness Biking

Remote mountain biking is different from regular mountain biking because you will be traversing isolated country where you may not cross paths with others at all during your day's ride. Consequently, you may have questions about how to do it safely. This section will help you prepare mentally and physically. We will discuss what equipment you will need, how to prepare your body to endure this challenge and the proper mental attitude. I will give you the best advice I can, based on the 33 years of hands-on fitness experience I've had.

I have no formal degrees, certificates or licenses that state I'm an expert. However, people who know me would say I'm an honor graduate from the School of Hard Knocks. You'll want to take what I offer, mix it with what you know, scramble in a few things the paper-experts say, and make a decision. I call it life.

You'll want to carry numerous items with you when you head into the big country. When I started biking off-roads in the southern tier, I only carried the clothes on my back.

As I continued to enjoy the rides, I systematically brought more essentials. Last year I finally gave in and bought a first aid kit. It took me six years and 8,000 miles to get to it. The wait was my stupidity.

What To Bring on Your Ride:
◈ **Gel Seat Cover**
A gel seat cover is an excellent addition—it will soften your ride.

◈ **Sheepskin Cloth Cover**
For even more comfort, you might add a sheepskin cloth cover with foam padding over the gel cover.

◈ **Seat**
A comfortable seat makes for a far more pleasant ride. For some rides, you will be on the bike as much as seven hours a day and possibly 12 or more if you encounter trouble. So you'll want to avoid injury from your seat, which could happen if you are riding for long periods.

The wilderness may mesmerize you and have you forgetting to watch for holes, ruts, rocks, etc. A sudden jar could cause an injury. People with even minor sciatica, disk or prostate irritations should consider the possibility of injury before getting on a bike.

I do not recommend remote mountain biking on a standard size seat. You should have a seat wide enough to ride comfortably as well as to protect nerves and organs. I'm not overstating this—it can be unsafe if you lose your ability to sit due to pain or injury.

You can die in the wilderness from something as simple as a bad seat. If you are unable to sit, coupled with managing your energy poorly, you *could* jeopardize your life. You could become exhausted and/or dehydrated from excessive standing on your pedals and walking. You tend to deplete energy quickly under such conditions, which may cause a panic attack. No matter how rugged you may be, "under parts" are soft, so protect them with a good seat.

❖ Computer Odometer

Serious riders already have one of these handy devices. Those of you who don't have one, I would strongly suggest you get one. When riding into unknown territory, you need to keep track of mileage, average speed and total trip-time.

If you are an extremely adventurous biker and know your whereabouts in the wilderness, then an odometer is optional. But everyone else will benefit significantly by using one. Traveling in the forest and depending on your intuition only, is risky business.

Venturing into areas where accurate maps are not available may present situations in which the woods can fool you. Topographical features in many areas look identical, which can be confusing for an inexperienced adventurer. If you are tired on top of it, you could find yourself making critical mistakes. You cannot depend on recollection, especially when it's your first trip to a region. If you guess which road to take, and go the wrong way, you may pedal for hours before you realize you chose the wrong road. It could be life-threatening especially if you have expended your energy reserve or you are lost.

Trekking with a computer odometer provides you with well-needed security. You can track your trip by noting miles at landmarks and intersections. You can scout off the track without guessing how far you have gone. The instrument allows you to plan your adventure based on the combination of terrain and distance. Subsequently, it helps you to learn your limitations. Finally, a major reason for owning an odometer is that it may help you survive to tell your stories.

❖ Tools

Tools such as vise grips, wrenches, screwdrivers, razor blades, jackknife, tube levers, chain breaker, appropriate spare hardware and pump are included in your supplies. They are never missed until you need them. I recommend carrying all the tools mentioned in order to repair your bike.

◈ Packs

These packs are my choice: waist pack, belt pack, expanding wedge pack and frame bag. You can carry tools, a patch kit, spare chain, hardware, knife, matches, compass, first-aid kit, marker tape, water, binoculars, extra socks, allergy pills, Motrin, Velcro strips, plastic bags, and spare tube in them. Also it's a good idea to carry a raincoat, winter hat, gloves and warm coat when the weather requires it.

Remember if you are forced to sleep in the woods over night, the temperature can drop drastically from daytime highs. Furthermore, weather conditions in the mountains and forests are unpredictable. Watch local forecasts and evaluate changes as they occur. Sometimes I will take a thermal cover when the risk of cold temperatures exists.

◈ Candy

You'll need to pack carefully for your wilderness rides because supplies like food, water and candy, will not be readily available. The closest store could easily be 50 miles away, so make sure you pack enough goodies.

Sometimes I gobble up a little candy within the first 10 minutes of the morning. However, I rarely take more than five Good-&-Plenty's at one time during the whole journey. Usually I eat a few every 45 minutes to an hour, depending on the various conditions of the run. I eat some the instant I feel weak or disoriented. Furthermore, I definitely have a bunch when my vision is affected. For example, if I squint and a blotch of light appears, it signals low blood sugar and I'll consume some sugar.

The tough part is picking out a kind of sugar that will agree with your body when you are perspiring heavily. Candy bars may be okay early in the morning when conditions are cool, but usually you don't need them until later when your blood sugar levels drop. But when you open your pack to melted chocolate, that's not pleasant.

There is no place to keep candy cool. In a closed pack, temperatures soar. In an open pack, it could fall out. In a waist pack, body sweat does a job on it. That's why I bring Good & Plenty's.

Good & Plenty's have almost no fat and are high in sugar content. The licorice is chewy and moistens a dry mouth. But the three most important benefits are they resist melting, they can be rationed, and they taste good. Also, they deliver a quick energy boost, which is ultra-important. I found the best way to carry them is in a pill bottle because no moisture gets inside.

◈ **Water or Sports Drinks**

How much water should you take on your journeys? Experts usually recommend that you drink lots of water to avoid dehydration. My recommendation is that you learn how much water your body needs before you go on a remote mountain bike ride—and take it from there. If you feel uncomfortable experimenting, then simply bring along extra water.

Which is better— water or sports drinks? After cranking thousands of miles in all kinds of weather and terrain, my experiences have led me to use both. If you have no candy, consume the sports drink.

I flood myself with water at night, drinking more in the morning before leaving. Then I make every effort to go dry until it's a must situation or I am headed back. I try to save some for emergencies. When I *do* drink, it's usually less than six ounces at a time. Traveling 30 or 40 miles without a gulp is not unusual for me. Know your own requirements.

◈ **Food**

In my opinion, eating food means you have to bring more water to aid digestion. When you factor in the energy drain from traveling by bike, you could be in energy deficit by the end of the day. So you may be better off bringing foods, such as bananas, apples, pears, that do not require a lot of water to aid in digestion. Do what works for you.

❖ Helmets

Today there are plenty of head gear options. My position on helmets can be answered in two words: personal preference. Experts recommend helmets because they save lives.

However, when you wheel yourself into the wilderness, you are on your own. The speed you travel, where you go, how far you go, the supplies you bring, what you wear, what you ride, when you ride and all other decisions are ultimately yours, as is your survival. That's why doing it is exhilarating and recharges the spirit!

❖ Maps

Remote mountain biking is adventurous, dangerous, thrilling—and uncertain. Let's talk about uncertainty.

The maps available in the North Country are anything but certain. Many snowmobile maps exclude roads that are not groomed. Some logging company's maps are confidential. Nevertheless, there are still a few good sources that make mountain biking runs special. In my opinion, the best available maps come from DeLorme Mapping Company. However, there are others. The list below provides additional resources:

DeLorme Mapping Company
P.O. Box 298
Freeport, ME 04032
(207) 865-4171

(This company has atlases for New Hampshire, Maine and Vermont. The map and guide series includes *White Mountain National Forest Map and Guide, Allagash and St. John Map and Guide, Illustrated Map of the Maine Coast; Moosehead Lake Map and Guide, Sebago Lake Region Map and Guide, Mt. Desert Island and Acadia National Park Map,* and the *Maine Map and Guide.*)

Hartnett House Map Publishers
P.O. Box 41
Freeport, ME 04032
(Rangely Lakes Region Map)

Boise Cascade Corporation
Shelburne, NH 03581
(207) 446-5268
(New England Region Recreation Map)

Maine Bureau of Parks and Recreation,
Snowmobile Division
(207) 289-3821

New Hampshire Division of Parks and Recreation
P.O. Box 856
Concord, NH 03301
(603) 271-3254

New Hampshire Department of Fish and Game Office
2 Hazen Drive
Concord, NH 03301
1-800-322-5018

Liebl Printing Company
Colebrook, NH 03576
(Inter-state Snowmobile Trail Map)

Spruce Cone Cabins
Route 3   P.O. Box 13
Pittsburg, NH 03592
(603) 538-6361
(Interstate snowmobile trail map—northern New Hampshire, Maine and Vermont)

United States Department of the Interior
US Geological Survey
Denver, CO 80225
(Provisional Quadrangle Maps)

◈ Compass

You should know how to use a compass. It's not difficult—it just takes a little practice. Don't buy one, put it in your pack and forget to use it until the day you are lost. Take the thing out and look at it once in a while.

A long time ago a man asked me how many compasses I should carry. I said one. He replied, "How could you be sure that it's working?" I said, "Okay, two." Then he asked, "If they both read differently, which would you believe?" I countered sheepishly, "Okay, three." Then he grilled, "Which two would you believe?" I answered, "The two that read the same." He snapped, "That leaves you with a 33 percent chance of getting lost. Are you happy with that?" I angrily retorted, "Yes," meaning no. Finally he quipped, "Then be sure your first one is working." I frustratingly replied, "How?" He directed, "Use it."

I will never forget that guy because he has saved my life many times over. But using it means something else. Use your compass on the trail. The goal is to know what direction you are traveling without using the compass. In order to have this wisdom you have to use it, as the man said.

Yes, there are ways to establish that the compass is working. One is simply going outside your home to verify north with what you know to be north. Also check the reading against the eastern summer sun in the morning or the western summer sun late afternoon. One check before you leave on your journey can easily satisfy your soul later in the woods.

Chapter 2

Mental and Physical Preparation

It Don't Come Easy

I feel somewhat uncomfortable about the number of times I have cautioned you. After all, the reason for the book is to introduce you to remote mountain biking, not scare you half to death. Yet, I don't want anyone to take this activity lightly. It's easy to buy a great bike and all the provisions necessary to ride. But being truly prepared is quite another story. We're talking between 30 and 70 miles per day on average, with some roads climbing steadily for as much as 10 miles. If you truly want to accomplish these types of rides, then you will need to train for it.

A balanced training program is critical. This includes biking uphill, pushing your bike uphill, walking, and most importantly, weight lifting. Additionally, stimulating the mind and getting adequate rest are important.

Many factors need consideration before you undertake this form of mountain biking. Know that there is more happening than what appears on the surface. Besides the obvious, physical tasks which mountain biking requires (such as standing while pedaling, pushing your bike uphill, leaning on the handlebars, and walking over, around or through rocks, downed trees and wet areas), there are also some mental challenges to endure. Mental challenges might include the ability to persevere through stressful events such as intense heat, driving rain or getting lost or all three at once.

Both the physical and mental components are equally fundamental to survival while biking in the wilderness.

Because mountain biking involves long distances and strenuous riding, you should train by biking. Running marathons will not prepare you for biking. Cross-training is good, but the best advice is to just get out there and do it! Start pedaling!

Although experts' opinions vary about what kind and the duration of cardiovascular conditioning one should have regularly—from 20 minutes a day three times a week to an hour a day five times a week—the underlying message is still: Do it!

Unfortunately, bike riding doesn't work that way. Even a stationary bike will not prepare you for tar roads much less dirt. Bike riding entails variable conditions and requires that you train within them. However, the concept of exercising at an elevated heart rate holds true. Do it on your bike—uphill. Remember, you are preparing for at least seven hours of steady time on the bike and perhaps as much as 12 hours.

A normal day of remote mountain biking will include numerous periods when you are required to perform cardiovascularly for at least 20 minutes. There may be times that you must do so for hours. So you need to train accordingly. The popular exercise regimen of three 20-minute workouts a week, won't cut it. The best training is to ride your bike—on tar to begin with. If you can pedal on tar roads on your mountain bike for the same distances you plan to ride on gravel, it'll be a good start. Obviously, use your mountain bike and not a road bike when you're training. Systematically increase your time on the seat as you get stronger.

When you are able to ride the same number of miles on tar as the off-road trails you'll ride, then mix your training day with some off-road stuff.

A Training Sampler

Here's a sample biking regimen that might be helpful to increase your endurance and get you into wilderness riding more quickly as well as being better prepared.

Let's use 50 miles off-road as your goal, and assume you have already reached that distance on tar with your mountain bike. Begin by riding in familiar territory with 10 miles on tar, then enter the woods for 10 miles and finish by doing another 10 on tar. Evaluate the difference in how you feel for the comparable 30 miles on tar. Consider any significant changes. Some important indicators to watch are tired muscles, pain, thirst, hunger, strength, weakness, hyper-alertness and stamina. If everything seems stable then adopt the route as a routine. If not, scale it down and try again.

Continue to vary the length of your rides, and intersperse your off-roads riding with tar-road travel until you feel secure about your capabilities.

Biking on dirt is probably twice as strenuous as tar. Yet it's difficult to speak in accurate terms about the comparison because of variables in terrain. Using this ratio, 50 miles of remote biking will tax your system equally to a 100-mile trek on tar. That's if you used a mountain bike for both.

Pushing Your Bike

It's good training to periodically get off your bike and walk it uphill. This prepares you for the real thing. Experiment with different hand positions on the handlebars to find what is most comfortable for you.

Walking

Walking is a substantial part of remote mountain biking. On a tough run you may find yourself hiking as much as 10 miles or more—uphill. So wear comfortable, supportive footwear. It is vitally important to have trained and hence, strengthened your legs and feet so they can carry you through the climb.

To train, find a long, steep hill where you can practice walking and pushing your bike. Wear the same shoes you would on a real trip and find a pace that suits you. Try various gaits and adopt one that allows you to continue moving steadily without experiencing pain. Be aware of your knees, ankles, hips and lower back. If something doesn't feel right, then change your gait. Sometimes a slight adjustment in your regular walking style can alleviate problems, too. Try walking on the other side of your bike. Try changing the position or the angle of your feet as they hit the ground. Try varying the height you lift your feet off the ground. Remember, it's all uphill and different from what you are used to. Experiment.

Pace Yourself

It is critical that you develop a comfortable walking gait because it may save your life. An awkward or uncomfortable gait can injure tendons or ligaments in the knee, foot or hip, which could slow your progress or terminate your ride completely. The pain could be so intense that you couldn't continue. Then you might be in danger from exposure or dehydration.

Make sure walking is part of your training regimen. If you will be biking where there are tough mountains or hills to deal with, then change your training route to include them. Do some heavy duty hiking to get in shape before you embark on remote mountain biking. Otherwise you may not be properly prepared to deal with this situation in the forest, and you will be at risk.

Hear Me Out

Attitude is everything. It's the strongest intangible factor in life. When you think mountain biking, you may immediately think of the high-intensity, reckless sport you see in magazines. Well, try this: Toss out the racing mania and substitute animal encounters. Transform the competition to recreation. Tear out the pictures in magazines of bikes flying over boulders, and substitute photos of wilderness scenes. Pedal gracefully into a well-balanced ecosystem instead of speeding by it without noticing. Try finding, rather than losing yourself.

47

If you want to become a remote mountain biker, you'll want to reconsider your attitude about speed. Remember the tortoise and the hare? The message is that attitude is a more efficient vehicle than skill. The tortoise won because he worked at it diligently, kept his pace and enjoyed the day. On the other hand, the rabbit went off track, was overconfident, and so came in second best.

When you explore the big country, ride slowly and allow nature to penetrate every fiber. To do this, keep your average riding speed around seven miles per hour (unless the terrain is flat or mostly descending).

In the past eight years my adventures have taken me through 10,000 miles of woods. Rarely did I average more than seven mph. Generally my journeys averaged 6.3 mph, which include speeds ranging from two mph (walking) to 35 mph (flying).

I believe attitude is everything because it reflects your outlook on life. What you think is what you get, it's as simple as that. If you head into the woods with a cocky attitude, proposing to know everything, you're in trouble. On the other hand, if you want to learn about the forest, then enter it humbly, persevere, make mistakes and ultimately accept your vulnerability. If you do it with this kind of mentality, you will learn much of what nature has to teach.

We are living in a shallow period of history. People are thinking from the outside instead of the inside, and it's extremely reckless. Today just because token trophies are awarded to those who have not earned or deserve them, don't get the idea that wisdom works the same way. Quite the contrary. Remote mountain biking can help you learn about yourself. If you are a weak person, it will surface, and you will be in for some tough pedaling. Don't worry, you'll be far better off by gaining one ounce of gritty spirit than a ton of gondola passes to the top, believe me.

Solo Rides

I enjoy biking alone. However, if it does not suit you to be by yourself, then find a partner or two. Both methods have advantages and disadvantages.

The obvious problem of biking solo is that there isn't any help if you get hurt, sick or your bike breaks down. Also, you could get lost and experience more trauma from fear than if you had companionship. In addition, some would say that two brains are better than one. Another possible shortfall, depending on how you look at it, is the fact that you must carry the total burden of risk, supplies and courage when you are alone.

But there are advantages to traveling in solitude. You have control of your day, which means you have total quiet and all the decision-making power. You will respirate less because you won't be gabbing all day—and so you won't dehydrate as quickly. You'll save energy by moving and resting at your own pace, and there won't be any temptation to compete. Also, there isn't any risk of encountering problems because your partners are unprepared. You won't collide with nor be sidetracked by other bikers. Finally, and most importantly, you can gain valuable insights about yourself while learning to become truly self-sufficient. The successes and failures become uniquely yours. Yes, it's a potent dose of reality.

Chapter 3

Getting Into Shape

Weight Lifting for Balance

In my opinion, weight lifting cannot be sufficiently learned by taking a few classes or by enrolling in a fitness program. It takes years of working out in the gym, performing different routines and committing long-term to an exercise regimen before real advances can be recognized. People should train in an injury-free environment that accommodates their individual needs and allows for steady progress. In addition, they need constant attention and coaching to assist them at perfecting the skills necessary for strength-building.

In this section I offer suggestions on strength-training to prepare for mountain biking. Again I have no certificates, but I do have 34 years of weight lifting experience. My philosophy may contradict what you already believe and that's okay because the more theories you hear, the more you learn.

There isn't anything worse than standing around in a weight room feeling completely ignorant while bodybuilders twice your size throw dumbbells around. It's kind of like being trapped on another planet where the average person has 400 pounds of muscle. Yet this is the best place for you to start. Here's what you do.

Walk around the exercise area and observe. Stop at every station where people are lifting and see how they are using the machines or barbells. Listen for different ideas. Jot down questions you have about what they are doing. Finally, bring your questions to an instructor and discuss a workout program.

Instructors need pertinent information before they can design your routine. They need to ask a myriad of questions. These questions need to be answered before a trainer can draft a preliminary workout regimen:

❖ 1. What physical activities have you engaged in during your lifetime?

❖ 2. Tell me when you were in the best and worst condition of your life?

❖ 3. How old are you and what is your present physical condition?

❖ 4. Talk to me about any injuries or pain and what you are doing about them or have done about them?

❖ 5. What do you want to accomplish through weight lifting?

❖ 6. How much time do you want to devote to the activity?

❖ 7. Can you perform regulation push-ups and pull-ups? How many?

❖ 8. What are your ideas on strength and stamina?

❖ 9. What is the longest time you have consistently worked out?

❖ 10. Where do you want to be in terms of progress toward your weight lifting goals in three months, six months, one year?

❖ 11. Describe any and all previous weight lifting experiences including pulley machines, home equipment, etc.?

❖ 12. Why are you seeking help in this area?

❖ 13. Do you have any bad habits that may affect your physical and mental condition?

❖ 14. If you have failed in the past at keeping up a regimen, tell me why you think you were unable to be consistent?

❖ 15. How many efforts have you failed on with regard to physical conditioning? Why?

❖ 16. How long did each of your attempts last?

Strength = Power + Endurance + Brainwork

Next you would want to try out on various machines and exercises. Depending on your experience level, the trainer will observe you while you perform exercises. A good trainer will continue to ask questions pertaining to your knowledge about weight lifting throughout the session. In turn, you should respond honestly and ask questions. Remember it's a two-way street. Beginners should never rush to build strength—it takes time for the body to adjust.

This is the formula that works for me: Strength = Power + Endurance. Every human has a unique muscle makeup. Just like we all have unique fingerprints. Weight lifting or other physical challenges work to change the mix of power and endurance tissues. In turn, strength is affected, and so the way I see it, your strength is directly proportional to the makeup of cells in each muscle. But this does not guarantee anything.

There is one thing missing in the formula: balance. In this context, balance means brainwork. Simply put, **Strength = Power + Endurance + Brainwork.** Muscles are regulated and disciplined by the brain. When the mind does the body justice, maximum strength-training can be attained. On the other hand, if the regulation is inadequate then output suffers or injury occurs. Finally, understanding that people are built differently, we need to make allowances to include many different workout regimens. It's not an exact science.

This is why balance is the most valuable intangible factor. We may have a strong genetic background, but if we abuse ourselves in wasteful and unproductive actions, then our strength is zapped, and with it, the fun. And the bodybuilding goal goes unaccomplished.

In my opinion, there are four major components to understand before you can progress at strength-training. Here they are in order of importance:

1. Stress
2. Technique
3. Time
4. Rest

Stress

Muscles simply do not grow beyond hereditary norms unless physical tasks are performed. But when asked to lift weight or do work, they respond accordingly by stimulating the exact amount of cells needed to complete the job.

You cannot fool your body. Suppose you call a pencil 100 pounds and lift it over your head for 25 repetitions. Did your muscles "see" the 100 pounds or one ounce? The answer is one ounce, of course. Because your muscles were not stressed beyond the *real weight* there was not any strength gain. On the other hand, 100 pounds of *real stress* to the muscles will bring into play all the cells necessary to do 100 pounds of work. *Real stress* is the key and most critical element to building strength. When muscles react to real stress, they adapt by thickening and becoming more dense.

Technique

The strength-building technique you use is key in determining whether muscles get the maximum amount of real stress. Let's say that you are military-pressing 100 pounds over your head and you jerk the bar upward by using momentum from bending your knees and arching your back. Do the muscles see 100 pounds? The answer is no. **You cannot fool your body.** The muscles detect the cheating motion by seeing less *real stress* and react as if it is less weight. However, if proper technique is used, then the muscles will "see" the total 100 pounds and respond by employing just enough cells to carry out the duty.

Keep in mind that you can do all your exercises perfectly, but if there is not enough weight to stress your muscles then they will not respond. The idea is to do your exercises using the correct form to ensure that the muscle groups being taxed are seeing the *real weight*.

Cheating is the biggest problem in weight lifting. Many lifters want to look stronger and purposely deviate exercises to change the *real stress* on their muscles and thereby give the illusion that they are lifting more. The muscles know better and employ the fewest number of cells, just enough to satisfy your brain. Cheating techniques defeat the purpose of strength training, and it's the single largest reason why people quit or get injured.

Time

The third concept is time. If you are stressing your system and working out with strict movements, you now need to pay attention to the amount of work done in a period of time. In other words, keep an eye on your rest periods between sets and total workout time. Weight lifting is a progressive activity. You will need to consider whether or not you should pick up the pace as you gain strength. In the beginning, 20 sets per workout should take you longer than after your body has adjusted to the routine. If you are consistently raising the weight, your rest periods or total workout time may not improve considerably, but that's okay. The difference will be noticeable by the additional workload to the system.

Rest

Last in the formula is rest. The body rejects too much work by using an internal mechanism that acts as an overload switch. If you go off the deep end and become addicted to your daily regimen, chances are you will overtrain. This causes the switch to activate and stop all progress. You'll get weaker and may even become ill, sustain an injury or lose muscle. If this happens the only way out is rest.

Keeping it Balanced

To maintain a balanced workout regimen—stress, technique, time and rest— must carry equal weight. You need to regulate the four in order to achieve a progressive strength-training program. Problems will arise if any of these components are not kept in balance.

Most serious lifters have experienced tough times in all areas before they have come to terms with them. That's why a graduate from even a certified school doesn't yet have the knowledge that took us "veterans" years to learn. This book cannot teach you how to read the body's signal system in order to hedge off potential difficulties from occurring. You have to live it to know it. You will never be perfect because the body is changing all the time.

Overtraining

Overtraining is without a doubt the most complicated and problematic dimension to understand about strength training. It creeps up on you and hangs around until you sway from your balanced philosophy. Then it'll sting you with a dose of stalemates, which can include sickness, sleepiness or sleeplessness, lack of energy, or a weakened body subject to injury. How do you know when you have overtrained? The answer is to learn your bodies signal system.

Listen to your instincts and be aware of your normal energy pattern. When things begin to change, your body sends a message to your brain. If you recognize the sensation early, take a day off. Stop exercising—even if you are in the middle of a workout session—often that's when you will get the strongest cue. If you act fast, you will hedge it off and recover before you weaken too much. Continue to overtrain and it could take months of low-key exercise to recoup.

Here are some common signs of overtraining:

◈ 1. An overwhelming desire to skip your workout.

◈ 2. Anxiety during the beginning stages of each workout session.

◈ 3. Finding yourself taking deep breaths frequently.

◈ 4. Periodic weakness during your workday hours.

◈ 5. When the weights feel heavier than usual.

◈ 6. Restlessness at night.

◈ 7. Emotional distress of varying degrees.

◈ 8. Hanging your head or arms as if they feel dead.

◈ 9. A cold coming on. Feelings that you may be getting sick.

◈ 10. Feelings of dehydration.

◈ 11. Unusually difficult to get up in the morning.

◈ 12. Desire to quit your routine.

◈ 13 Guilt over bad workouts.

◈ 14. Feeling psychologically dependent on the workout regimen.

◈ 15. Little progress or some digression in training.

◈ 16. Workout times expand or inter-set rest periods expand.

There are some solutions to overtraining as well. First, strive to maintain a balanced approach so that you will not get into trouble. Have rest periods strategically built-in to your program and be flexible, varying times until you find an acceptable situation. Try to keep on a consistent schedule—so your body and mind can adjust. Never workout on "no workout" day. Remember, **rest is the silent strength of all routines and regimens**.

Second, enjoy your time away from the regimen. Don't go to the club for any reason on your day off. Do something you greatly enjoy. If you are doing something that makes you happy, your body and mind will re-energize. Don't run a marathon on your weekend rest period. However, if you like to walk in the woods, hunt, fish or boat, then go for it.

Practice, Practice, Practice

Finally and most importantly, practice makes perfect. You might have to experiment with various methods to combat overtraining syndrome. Light days mean lowering the weight for all exercises. Preprogrammed light days are the best because you know they are coming in advance, which is a psychological and physical boost. Switching or substituting exercises can retain your interest, and save energy. Furthermore, periodic changes in the total routine will give burnt-out tissue time to revitalize, while different muscle cells take over. Programs that include built-in cycles are best.

My experience indicates that the body strengthens in cycles of three to eight weeks, depending on the individual. This simply means you gain strength in blocks of time between three and eight weeks, as long as you are taking a balanced approach. Some of you remember looking in the mirror and seeing new ripples showing up. If you checked the calendar it was probably about three weeks after you began your routine. Usually your system needs at least this long to respond to a change in the workload. The mistake most people make is thinking they can steadily progress without any time off.

When the body gets stronger, it's changing. When it changes, it needs time to adjust. If you train hard during these adjusting periods, the automatic protection system switches on and stops everything. If you still continue, overtraining syndrome kicks in and subtracts the gains you have worked so hard for. Therefore, it's essential to design a program that allows the body to be strengthened, while also providing time to adjust to changes. Using a cyclical approach is the only way to go.

Weight Training Workout Regimen

The cyclical process in weight lifting involves three phases in which endurance and power routines are interspersed. In the first segment (two weeks) you gradually intensify your workout to prepare for the second phase. Push yourself during weeks three and four, backing off slightly (10-15 percent) for the remaining two weeks, of the designated six-week schedule. If the program was designed to complete a cycle every eight weeks, then the second phase would be four weeks, with the first and third phases remaining the same. When you finish the six- or eight-week regimen, a corresponding six- or eight-day rest is mandatory. Begin a new six- or eight-week schedule by using the same weight amounts used in the last phase of your previous cycle. Here's a scenario for just one exercise, but it will hold true for the total routine.

Week 1: Bench Press 100 pounds

Week 2: Bench Press 105 pounds

Week 3: Bench Press 115 pounds

Week 4: Bench Press 125 pounds

Week 5: Bench Press 110 pounds

Week 6: Bench Press 110 pounds

Week 7: Rest-rest-rest-rest-rest-rest for six days!

Week 8: Bench Press 110 pounds

Week 9: Bench Press 115 pounds

Week 10: Bench Press 130 pounds

Week 11: Bench Press 140 pounds

Week 12: Bench Press 125 pounds

Week 13: Bench Press 125 pounds

Week 14: Rest-rest-rest-rest-rest-rest for six days

You can see that a balanced program will allow segments for moderate, intense and scaled-back training sessions. The scaled-back segment (weeks 5 and 6) is just backing off the peak activity level occurring in weeks 3 and 4. This allows your system to adjust by giving the muscles time to thicken. A rest period gives your stressed body valuable time to regenerate. When you begin the new sessions you are fresh and can easily work your way into moderate training while preparing to explode during the middle phase.

This cyclical pattern is how your body builds strength. Take my advice, go with the flow of your own energy level while systematically improving your endurance. At the same time, enjoy and take your rest seriously. You will need all of it when you remote mountain bike. There is absolutely no way I could do it without weight lifting for upper body strength.

My Favorite Routine

Here's my favorite upper body routine. Go for it!

1. Dumbbell bench press

2. Standing military press

3. Lat bar pull downs—wide grip

4. Lat bar pull downs—close grip

5. Dumbbell shoulder shrugs

6. Dumbbell curls

7. Tricep push downs

8. Standing tricep extensions

9. Stomach crunches—I hate them, too!

10. Leg raises (optional)

Chapter 4

How to Remote Mountain Bike

Life Parallels

Life is tough. Everyone bears scars. Yet there are moments of glory, resilience and happiness. Mountain biking in the wilderness is also tough. But there are those same moments of glory. Traveling alone in remote territory can be equated to our burden on earth. We all experience, fail, grow. But always we strive to do better. In the woods, you will feel everything from insecurity to exuberance. The ultimate quest is to reach that peace that lies deep within. Do your best and let the struggle be your reward.

The Night Before

The first task to accomplish the night before you leave to drive to the North Country for a long bike ride, is to eat well. Then set your clothes out and load your gear packs. At dawn you won't want to waste time scavenging for supplies. Also you may be fuzzy-headed in the morning, causing you to forget supplies that could save your life later in the day. You might want to pack your vehicle in advance.

Study Your Maps

Along with maps of the area you will be riding in, include maps of outlying areas also—just in case you get lost or decide to deviate from your planned route. Scan the topography. Make note of mountain peaks, valleys and watersheds. Pay close attention to the natural landmarks based on your intended compass heading. In other words, if you are traveling northwest, recognize that a stream, lake or mountain should appear as you ride. This can give you confidence as well as bearing identity. While you are studying maps at night, overload on water even if you need to get up a couple of times during the night.

Double check everything before you head out to the starting point, and be careful not to leave your bike behind.

The Starting Point

Before you shove off on your trek, here are a few tips you should know before pedaling into the woods. Take your time mounting the packs on your bike. Make certain everything is tightly attached. Double check your water, candy, computer and compass, as well as other supplies. If you take medication, remember to bring it along. Check your tires for air pressure and adjust them to your liking. When you crank 50 miles or more, tire pressure can affect your energy level. Also, get used to knowing how much air is in the tires by squeezing them instead of using a pump gauge. Take care of your bike—it's your best friend out there. Adjust your seat for comfort. Inspect the chain and all hardware. Decide if you should bring rain gear or warm clothes—based on how the weather looks. Finally, don't forget maps, money, license and keys, before locking your car. Oh yeah, don't forget to set your computer odometer at zero.

Beginning the Adventure

The best advice in this whole book is: "**Take it easy. Don't rush or compete.** Think steady." The worst thing you can do is to begin the day with hard-nosed pedaling. Instead, let your body and mind adjust to the silence of the morning by sneaking into the forest. Go slowly, methodically, quietly and blend in with the landscape. In this way you will fine tune your senses much like an animal.

If the road gradually descends in the beginning, good. Just roll along without pedaling and feel how everything accepts you. Travel at four or five miles an hour and you will begin to experience nature at its finest.

If the road gradually ascends in the beginning, it's well it does, too. Just pedal as if you were rolling at four or five miles an hour. All the while concentrate on becoming aware of the ecosystem around you—the air, smells, colors and sounds. Be part of it.

If the road steeply ascends in the beginning, that's no big deal. Work calmly at climbing until you can't do it without straining, then get off and walk your bike. Look around you as you push your bike. Don't think, just feel.

If the road steeply descends in the beginning, use your brakes and crawl forward. Totally commit yourself to the wilderness. The day is yours.

Accept Randomness
Mountain Biking is exciting enough in and of itself, but it's even more exciting if you leave your worries behind. Have fun.

Remember you will not be an expert your first time out. It takes time to learn. And even after you know how, you can encounter difficulties. Your success rate depends a lot on attitude. Think positive, and act positive. The trick is to ride without any expectations. Don't fret about what you can't control. Accept that in life there is randomness.

You can't plan, formulate or anticipate everything. Let it go, say "the hell with it," and enjoy the risk of living. You're not going to win over random events, because they're unpredictable. When you think about it, you will agree that randomness is just another word for newness. The whole idea of knowing what is new immediately destroys the fun. You can't be excited about opening a gift when you know what's inside, right? So, believe in the now and your mind will stay alert.

Remember the feeling you got as a kid when you first learned to ride your bike or swing? Wow! Remember that? You were discovering. Well, when you are in the woods, notching forward on your machine, let the same wonder overcome your being. Discover. It's the key to feeling spectacular and an answer to living in the present without worrying.

Traversing Short-Rise, Short-Fall Terrain

After biking over 10,000 miles since 1988, I have to say that riding on short rise-and-fall terrain is easiest—because the roads or trails are generally rolling up and down without steep climbs. The reason they are easy is that once you climb the first hill, momentum carries you part way up the next. Each successive ascent is accomplished without a lot of energy. When you experience this kind of momentum on hills, expect your average rate of speed to increase two to three mph. Occasionally the ups and downs gradually ascend, but the strain is minimal.

Sometimes the physical features of land work to your advantage. One highlight that you will probably enjoy on your journeys, is riding through marshy areas teeming with wildlife. Rounding a curve often unfolds an animal scene just ahead on the path. Curving roads also have the advantage of breaking the wind, so you don't have to fight against it for extended periods.

Traversing Steep Ground

Traversing steep territory on a 50-mile run could mean climbing for a significant part of the journey. A fair estimate might be up to six hours of an eight hour trip. The most laborious runs generally include upward-sloping terrain, with intermittent high-rise ascents from one to three miles.

For example, if you pick a loop that circles up and around a mountain, you could be cranking almost all the time, depending on your return route. Evaluate in advance whether you can handle the strain.

The best way to cope with this topography is to push your bike at a steady pace. Keep moving even if you slow down. Look ahead instead of down, so you don't get motion sickness. Find a grip on the handlebars that conserves energy. You may want to switch sides occasionally as you push forward, too.

Rest is important. I never lie down; and rarely do I sit on the ground. Instead I will find a boulder or stump and lean against it. Usually I lean on my seat or stand and listen to the quiet until my energy returns. Mostly though, I keep moving so I can spend time enjoying animals when I encounter them. Remember, the turtle never races, and rests infrequently. That's me.

My recommendation is that you avoid crumpling into a precarious position that may result in a pulled muscle or joint injury when tugging yourself up.

To climb a steep hill, work at a steady pace. When you *do* reach your limit, get off and push your bike until you can ride again. Don't start riding in the middle of an uphill climb. You are better off walking the difficult section and conserving energy.

Trudging up mountainous roads demand a great deal of stamina that could lower your blood sugar to dangerous levels. Have plenty of candy and an adequate water supply so you can keep pedaling when the times get tough. Think about how you will maintain your energy level throughout the day. Figure each journey on a 12-hour basis, even if you have only planned an 8-hour adventure. Anything can happen. Reserve some energy in case of problems.

Here are some tips for conserving energy: Strip down to limit sweating, even if it means being a bit chilly. Drink six or eight ounces of water at a time. Leave at dawn and travel the majority of miles before the sun is too intense. Wear a cap with a visor. It keeps the sun from your face and conserves energy.

Climbing to high ground means there will be plenty of descents. Make sure you track your whereabouts—intersections look different when you fly past at 25 or 30 miles an hour. You can easily lose your way if you don't slow down and look for clues about your turn. Also it helps to keep an eye on your odometer as you labor upward. So you will know how far it is back to that point. If it's a mile, than you don't have to slow down until you get close to that distance.

Finally, be aware that touring steep mountain country is quite taxing to your system. Don't plan two or three back-to-back journeys of 50 miles or more in this territory unless you are 100 percent sure you can do it. A second day can leave you with far less stamina than the first. Don't take things for granted. If you do plan a number of successive timberline trips, eat like a hog at night to restore the calories you have burned—you'll need them for biking this kind of terrain. Also drink lots of water each evening and before heading out at sunrise.

Negotiating Long, Slow Ascents

In remote New Hampshire you travel roads that never seem to stop rising. Some trails snake upward for 15 or 20 miles. These runs are enjoyable because the trip back is cake and ice cream. Yet traversing long, slow ascents has its peculiarities.

Your muscles can cramp. Sitting and working the pedals for four hours or more can tighten certain body parts. It can limit blood-flow as well. If your hips, buttocks, lower back, calves or thighs feel uncomfortable, alternate standing and sitting. The best advice, though, is to occasionally walk your bike.

Fatigue or exhaustion can occur if you hurry on the slow grades, so take it easy. Pace yourself so that your breathing is even and not strained. Keep moving though, and vary the speed of travel according to how you feel.

Cranking toward higher elevations can burnout your upper body, too. Holding onto your handlebars while gradually climbing for a long distance requires more effort than most other terrain does. To stave off fatigue, equalize your grip, and make sure you pull evenly on the handlebars. Let each side carry its fair share of the burden and you won't weaken or develop tendinitis. Hands, shoulders, biceps, triceps, forearms, back, obliques, stomach, and even the chest muscles, are acting in unison when you are biking.

Remote mountain biking requires a great deal of upper body strength.

The torso also plays an important part in your success when wilderness riding. Think about it. You are holding yourself up for hours—pulling, pushing, gripping, keeping your head elevated, taking the shocks, twisting, leaning, turning and carrying your weight—all with your upper body.

The current fad is to keep your seat high, forcing you to hunch over the handlebars, road-bike style. In this awkward position, the legs do most of the work. However, it's ridiculous to think you can be comfortable when traveling this way eight to 12 hours a day. If you do it, you're asking for trouble because you may over-stress your lower back causing spasms. And then what?

A more upright position is far more comfortable for long rides. People say that I look like the Wicked Witch of the West because of the way I sit upright in the seat. It may look funny but what's important is to be comfortable and to ride without risking injury.

Riding in Adverse Conditions

Mountain biking is tough even when land conditions are not challenging. Soft gravel, swamp puddles, roots, rocks, tractor moguls, tire-grooved roads, muck, mud and grass can affect your journey. Add to that rain, wind, heat and cold. But listen, if you're adventurous, you'll welcome these variables and do fine as long as you keep a level head.

Suppose a wind and rain storm kicks up suddenly when you have 25 miles to go. Stop riding, evaluate how much energy you have left, and estimate how much longer it will take you to complete the trip. Check supplies, prepare to ration them, and calculate how you will do it. Then work your plan—moving at a steady pace according to your energy reserves. Remain calm. Consider shortcuts only if you're sure about them. My experiences prove that the long way is usually the sure way.

Words to the Wise

◈ Don't be fooled by the false security of tire-grooved ruts, especially going downhill. Avoid them because they can dump you off your bike.

◈ Avoid rushing into unknown puddles if you want to stay on the seat. Get off and walk the bike through or around them. You don't know what surprises may be hiding under the surface.

◈ Don't hop your bike over downed trees or boulders. They can be deadly encounters. Go around obstacles when possible or get off and carry your wheels over them.

◈ Firmly grip the handlebars with at least one hand when crossing streams. Hold the bike with both hands if you are walking it. If you are hopping from rock to rock, pull the bike by the handlebars with the hand farthest away (palm forward) while keeping it steady with the closest hand.

◈ Avoid speeding through tall grass on a downhill ride. Hidden rocks or holes can throw you before you have time to react.

◈ Ride beside tractor moguls. Traveling over this stuff jars your bones to death. You can even get motion sickness on this rough ground. If you should vomit in the heat, you chance becoming dehydrated. Plus the shaking could cause an injury.

◈ Keep both hands on the bars when you are clocking downhill. If your cap flies off in the wind, stop and get it, but never hold it on your head while you are descending. It's too dangerous. Likewise, avoid taking a drink, wiping away tears caused by the wind, adjusting a pack, stretching or waving to a fisherman. Hold on.

◈ Watch for washed-out or caved-in areas on the road. Also, metal culverts work themselves up through the gravel and offer quite a bump on an otherwise smooth-sailing surface. If you are looking around enjoying the day, that's okay, but slow down or you may be picking rocks from your teeth. If you are a guy, things could get pretty sore down below, if you accidentally hit a pot hole.

◆ Bogs will slow you down. So go around them—unless you want to lose your shoes and smell like a moose for a week.

◆ Expect to sweat if you go hauling yourself down soft graveled mountain trails. Things may be fine while you are descending, but returning is a different story. Every mile you wander over soft dirt is multiplied by two if you return the same way. Be sure you are strong enough for it.

◆ Don't test loose gravel at 30 mph. Slow down. Gravel works like brakes—and you could come to an immediate halt.

◆ Watch for upcoming wooden bridges. Sometimes tires will fall between slats. Travel on the dirt-filled area. If you are worried, slow down or walk.

◆ Swamp grass and mud can drain energy—it's like riding through peanut butter. Walk through it.

◆ Don't worry about forging through small brooks and streams during low-water days. If it's summer, a bit of dampness won't bother you.

◆ **Perspective is everything. Expect panic to surface if conditions turn against you. Recognize its presence and carry on. In remote country you can't afford to play games on your bike. Your purpose is to tour the wilderness, observe the wildlife and enrich your spirit. Do it safely.**

Mastering the Skills

Balance was the key to learning how to ride when we were kids. Several falls later, pedaling was as easy as walking. Soon you were traveling the neighborhood by bike. What a high that was. Remember searching for two-cent bottles, finding one and scooting to the store for a couple of big Bazooka bubble gums? Whaahoooo, those were the days.

Anyway, you will feel the same sensation when you embark on your first remote-athon. As in yesteryear, your task will be to master the skill of balancing.

So make sure you prepare physically, mentally and emotionally. You must manage all of them to be successful at remote mountain biking. Let me explain by presenting a realistic scenario without nature encounters.

The Real Thing

Let's say you are prepared for a 50-mile run. It's your third long ride (50 miles) in the wilderness.

Segment One

The morning is cold for early July, 30 degrees, but not unusual for northern New Hampshire. You have mapped a route, estimated distances and are starting out with a breeze at your back. It's new territory and you are energetic, positive and keen. The terrain is steep so you stand on your pedals for the first couple of miles. Midway up, you peel down to a T-shirt to avoid profuse sweating, and conquer the rise to find yourself on a high point overlooking a valley and river. Here, you stop to look through binoculars while your heart pounds in the silent, foggy morning. Before you shove off, you glance back at the mountain, feeling victorious that you conquered it on your bike.

Segment Two

The views are spectacular as you glide downhill for the next six miles. There are a few intersections, but you follow what appears to be the main road. When you reach lower land the gravel road splits sharply to the right, which you take without pulling the map from your pocket. You say, "I will remember this to be a left when I return," and continue descending into marshlands. A four-way corner materializes. This time you check the map but find that there isn't such a corner shown. Well, it's no big deal because you know the region's maps are not current. You turn left because there is more open country in this direction and you are sure you will remember how the scene looks when you return.

70

Segment Three

Finally, the ground levels off. Mile after mile whizzes past as you advance into a more and more remote area. It is easy rolling and you feel strong, pushing onward past roads branching left and right. You cruise past tall trees. The sun warms the dirt under your bike. You stop and gulp a full bottle of water. It feels so good going down you can't stop drinking and say, "Ah, what the hell, I've got plenty of energy for today." The odometer indicates you have traveled more than three hours and 23 miles already today. The exercise high is kicking in—just in time for the next mountain range.

Segment Four

The ascent is gradual at first but ends snaking steeply for the final three miles. You have to walk nearly all of it. The view is tremendous as the road continues on top of a ridge. (Ridge roads are great because they offer an unobstructed view.) You check the odometer and find you have covered 27 miles. That's more than the 25 planned but you don't care. As you pause to think about notching ahead, a large bull moose runs across the next rise. That settles it, the encounter is on. The moose runs toward another moose and they trot ahead of you on the road. You follow for a mile until they split off into the brush. The excitement has you wandering a bit farther in the hot, open sun. At mile 30, you turn and start back.

Segment Five

Suddenly you notice a dark front edging the horizon. You rush, planning to gobble up ground before bad weather sets in. Immediately, you are pressing against a 20 mph wind. You press against it and move forward. At the top of the ridge you feel relief because the grade turns in your favor for the next four miles. However, going against the ever-increasing wind is giving you the jitters. You also think about the 23 miles left to go. You have never done 60 miles, and suddenly you feel drained.

Segment Six

Soon you are lightly rolling along. However, the combative wind persists. Still, you press forward. Clouds are starting to cover the sky, but the sun remains out, causing the sweat to flow in spite of the cooling breeze. You feel a twinge of pain in your right hip every revolution of the crank. It's due to excessive straining and you reluctantly stop. Then you notice the odometer is reading two miles. The sweatshirt tied to the handlebars must have slid over and hit the reset button. You will have to function from memory from here on.

Segment Seven

At the four-way intersection, your exhilaration turns to panic. Your memory fails you. Nothing looks familiar. You ride circles in the intersection. Then stop, lean on your seat and think. You spin around trying to recognize the direction from which you just came. Panic intensifies while you struggle to gain composure, but the truth is, you are lost. As your heart races, you concentrate on recalling the morning scene. Was it a right or left?

Segment Eight

In a burst of insight, you turn right. Wheww! It's the correct direction. However, your water is gone and you are exhausted. Heavy breathing forces you to slow the pace even though clouds have taken over and rain is imminent. You glance toward the mountain to your left. The mountain's presence confirms your position. Your confidence returns.

Segment Nine

You push the bike uphill for 15 minutes and stop. You notice the sky has returned to blue. Fifteen minutes later and the sun is bearing down. The wind retreats a bit. You can't believe how strenuous it is to keep moving. The next six miles are mostly by foot, causing your Achilles tendons and hips to cry out. Two hours later you coast toward the car. You made it—60 miles in 11 hours.

Reflections on the Scenario
Segment One
Standing and pedaling for the first two miles was too much strain on the system too early. You should have walked some of it.

Thinking that you conquered the mountain was off the mark. You shouldn't be competing, there is no need. Challenging yourself is okay, but you don't "win" over nature.

Segment Two
Cruising through intersections without stopping can be foolish unless distinctive landmarks exist. You were caught up in the thrill of descent and avoided doing what would have saved you a lot of grief later on in the day. Because if you become lost, you will wish you had marked your trail.

Never depend on your memory in new territory. The scene appears differently when you approach it from another direction. Four-way corners always need to be marked. We will cover that shortly.

Segment Three
You were relieved when the ground leveled off. Try staying neutral emotionally about the terrain no matter how tough or easy it is to ride.

You were pushing too hard for no apparent reason other than you felt strong. You were rushing for no reason.

Giving in to your thirst may come back to haunt you. Ration it so you have enough throughout the day. Don't be greedy. Balance takes discipline.

Thinking short term is not OK in remote territory. Be cognizant of distances traveled and time expended, especially in new country.

Beware of the exercise high, it can make you cocky and interfere with decision-making. Manage it right.

Segment Four

Going farther than planned is all right as long as you are alert to the risks. Know your limits and stretch them moderately. Never go overboard. You could end up a dead hero.

Segment Five

Worry gets you nowhere and it consumes valuable energy. Remain calm. You will think better.

Working or exercising at a stable pace is best for long-term stamina. If you feel drained, you are probably overworking. Slow down a little, have some candy and/or water and regain your energy. Rest in the shade.

Segment Six

Slow down when you feel pain. If it continues, rest. In any case you have to manage it. Never give up and wait for help, because it may not come in remote lands.

Don't tie clothing to handlebars unless they can be secured without affecting the odometer.

You may not have taken enough water. Relax, panic is starting to take over.

Segment Seven

Memory lapses come when you are keyed-up emotionally. Sometimes low blood-sugar causes light-headedness. Eat a piece of candy and drink a little water. Relaxing may refresh your memory.

Never circle around an intersection with a bike. Instead, lay it down just before the intersection facing the direction from which you came. So at least you will know what direction you came from. This method also allows you to bushwhack or scout off the trail. When you return, the bike will give you bearing.

Segment Eight

Control your emotions. If you panic, you are not in control. Indecision is counterproductive.

The journey is not over until you reach the car. Don't set yourself up for disappointment by anticipating.

Segment Nine

Expect weather changes. Listen to reports before you head out. Remember, showers come and go quickly. No need to change your plans because of a little rain.

Remember the sun causes heat radiation on gravel roads, which in turn warms you. Wind is unpredictable—accept it.

Take everything as it comes. Stay in the present. Always be prepared and willing to persevere through one more shot of adversity.

Be prepared to push your bike up many miles of tough mountainous terrain. Keep going, just as you do in life.

Maintaining Stamina

Maintaining stamina is nothing more than staying the course—whether it's mountain biking, fitness training, rearing a family, working for wages, overcoming an injury, going to school or competing in a sport.

To build and maintain stamina, you need to keep yourself physically fit. The more biking you do, the more stamina you build. Knowing your body's capabilities will keep you strong in the long run, so learn to perform at various levels and intensities.

Practice riding for the many situations you will encounter. Stay seated for long rides, stand for others, "burn" on hills, travel fast, travel slow, vary the gears, push, wade, grind, and finally, negotiate middle ground for all of them. Also, while you are experiencing these various situations, strive to balance the workload so each muscle group is working at the same tempo.

This takes concentration, which is what is missing for people who have trouble maintaining energy. Each side of the body must do its share. The trouble starts when there is an imbalance—which results in an overload to certain muscles.

Find a spot on every revolution of the crank that will accommodate rest, even if only for a fraction of a second. Use your upper body to complement the lower. Divide the burden. That way you will relieve muscles that are doing too much work. They will respond by giving you more total output. The result will be a balanced system that performs efficiently and regenerates as it goes.

In a way, learning to remote mountain bike is comparable to fitting together pieces of a puzzle. Sometimes the pieces are easy to locate while other times elusive. Consider reading this book slowly and at least a couple of times. Pool the information you learn with your existing knowledge, visualizing each section until you begin to see the whole picture. When the total scene unfolds, you will be better prepared to shove off on a wilderness mountain biking adventure.

Riding Under Pressure

There will be days when you have a mechanical breakdown, develop an injury, get lost, go farther than planned or lose track of time. Any of these circumstances could cause you to ride like hell to escape the wilderness before dark. If this happens, here's what you do.

First, stop and think. Estimate how many miles you need to travel to return to your car. Calculate the average speed you are apt to travel based on the terrain you are traveling on. If it's mountainous terrain, you can count on long, moderate climbs. Gradual terrain would present flat to moderate pedaling. Steep terrain requires you to push your bike.

When you push because of time restraints, the pressure is on. Stay cool, alert, and most of all, balanced in the approach you take to overcome adversity. The goal is to make it back before dark, but if it doesn't happen, you are better off late and living, then dead on time.

A few extra tips about this kind of riding: increase your speed on the gradual terrain instead of the tough ascents. Otherwise, you will burn a lot of energy and cover little ground. Choose terrain that requires the least effort—you will make faster time. Use momentum at every opportunity. Let the hills do some of the work for you. Finally, recognize that you are your own best asset.

Selecting a Plan

Before entering the remote wilderness, choose a plan. Following are 10 options. The goal is to match your capabilities with your intentions. You may be capable of completing all these plans or just a few. In any case, the hints described here should help you select which ones are best for you.

Plan 1

Biking for mileage only. Having no specific route. Example: To ride a 50-miler, making decisions as you go.

This plan works when you know the territory, but can be dangerous because you may get lost. With mileage as a goal, you may rush off into difficult riding areas. Terrain is everything—sometimes a 30-mile run is harder than a 60. Monitor your energy level, so you can make sound decision as to whether to go on or turn back. This is a good plan if you are building stamina, otherwise stay away from it.

Plan 2

Having a specific destination in mind—unfamiliar with route.

Bring maps that include areas on the perimeter of your route. Carry extra supplies if you are apprehensive. Travel slower than if you knew the territory. Be careful on the descents when your view is obstructed by corners.

Check maps and compass frequently. Mark every road. Ration supplies. Keep in mind—tomorrow is another day. Great plan if you're capable—this is what it's all about.

Plan 3
Having a definite destination in mind—familiar with route.

You know the territory but things can still go wrong. Always bring adequate supplies. Stick to your plan and fight the temptation to travel farther than planned. Have fun but take all normal precautions. Great run—no worries about direction, just ride.

Plan 4
Bike scouting. Discovering unexplored terrain. Investigating all side roads and trails.

Whaaahooo! This is new territory. But you can become confused easily, so be aware and alert, and mark your trails. Identifying intersections is important. Mark every one.

Scouting is great, but do it systematically. Keep track of mileage and time. Travel the same road until it changes or dead ends. Great plan especially when weather is cooperative.

Plan 5
Return trip. Been there before but not sure of route.

You have traveled the area once, so pedaling this time will be somewhat familiar. But don't let memories give you a false sense of security. Check your maps and compass, and mark as you go.

Pace yourself. You may want to investigate roads you missed the first time. But stick to the plan.

Bring enough supplies even if the previous trip was easy. Weather conditions can change radically. Take mental notes of the landscape's features and peculiarities as you travel and compare them to your map.

Plan 6

Anything-goes biking. Includes bushwhacking. Example: All terrain is game—road, path, muck, rock, bush, water, tall grass, mountains, swamps—you name it.

Do this on a high-energy day. Usually it is best reserved for the first run of a series. Make sure you have had at least 72 hours of non-biking activity before you try this one.

Be prepared to face the harshest conditions of mountain biking. Stay cool even if you get wet and muddy. Bring extra bug repellent and socks. A baseball cap keeps the horseflies out of your hair. This plan means you are willing to bike on all terrain and face unknown challenges.

Plan 7

Photo day. Bringing a camera for photo opportunities.

This plan accommodates a shorter travel day because you will spend time taking pictures.

Strap the camera down so it doesn't bounce around. Don't bike with it hanging from your neck. A big camera can be cumbersome. If you're going to high country, take it easy on the descents—you don't want to damage your camera.

This plan is for photographing the views and wildlife that you may encounter.

Plan 8

Hanging out for encounters. Not much traveling. Goal is to see wildlife and experience the scenery.

A short traveling day. Take supplies along when you head into the bush to observe animals—early mornings and evenings are the best times for sightings. However, you might see creatures any time if you are quiet and blend in with the landscape.

Be careful if you bushwhack because you can easily get lost just 100 feet from the road. Take a compass bearing and check your maps before heading off on foot. Patience pays dividends. Animals see motion. So move slowly or not at all.

This plan is super when you need a break from the more strenuous ride.

Plan 9

Select terrain biking. Only interested in certain kinds of riding for the day. Example: Gradual, mountainous, moderate mix, all road, no muck, no streams, etc.

A great plan when you know the area and want to bike under familiar conditions. A relaxed situation because you have already made decisions and won't stray from your plan.

Plan 10

"No plans" adventure. Biking in the wilderness totally free from constraints or plans. Every decision is spur of the moment. This plan usually ends up being one of the other nine, but is not pre-planned.

Freedom! Ride anywhere you want. Just remember to ride responsibly.

Prepare as if you were carrying out Plan 2.

Have fun whatever option you choose!

Staying Alert

Mountain biking is a fully engaging, wondrously productive, tremendously challenging, spiritually uplifting and harmoniously gratifying activity! A bit overstated perhaps, but what else in your life could occupy free hours or days in such a positive and enriching manner?

Let's move on and cover another important part of wilderness biking—staying alert. You will be on dirt roads for many hours where you may find it challenging at times to remain alert and focused. As you pedal on, your mind can wander, which can have negative consequences.

The most significant reason is that you will drift from the present into the past. Don't allow it. Instead, concentrate on now. While you are discovering and learning, you are simultaneously delving into the moment at hand. Living in the present keeps you tuned into nature, where you just might experience what the word "awesome" truly means.

The problem with letting yourself mentally wander is that you significantly increase the chances of being lost or making mistakes. When you roll along in a daze, time, distance and direction are hard to judge. You do not want to lose your bearings in the forest, especially if the area you are traveling in is unfamiliar.

Letting your mind wander can cause confusion, which can be terrifying if you are lost in the forest. Here is a realistic scenario:

The day meets your every expectation. Weather conditions are perfect. Even the road requires only minimal effort. The landscape is spectacular. Suddenly you are jarred awake by a random thought—or maybe it was that rut in the road. Where am I? How many intersections have I traveled? I know I passed a left up there—I think. Why am I heading east? I have traveled 12 miles? It can't be. I just started (...son of a gun!). I need to turn around and return to something I recognize so I can get my bearings.

Believe me even if you have thousands of miles under your belt, this situation can happen to you. However, there is a way to avoid this scenario. But you have to exercise discipline. To solve this problem, stop at all tributary roads and mark them before going on. If there are no spur (side) roads, you don't have to worry about direction, but you will need to track time and distance. You need a system or a method to remain aware.

Discipline and Grit

Wilderness biking will help you find, or build, character. You must be humble in the backwoods. You will need to think differently than you do in the city. To be a part of the forest, you need to adapt and fit in. An isolated forest environment quickly proves that nature does things her way. Don't underestimate that.

You are a guest of Mother Nature. Secondly, you need to feel comfortable about the loss of control. Then, and only then, will your experiences be gratifying.

Beating the odds or more appropriately, living in harmony with nature, improves dramatically if a number of areas are addressed. We have already discussed the importance of being prepared physically.

Mental preparation is equally important. Let's look at this scenario. You are 30 miles from nowhere and without warning, the weather turns bad—rain. The road turns soft and a steep ascent is dead ahead on the trail. So you call upon your inner reserves to help you stay focused, and you press forward. You recall from past experience that adversity is easier to overcome when you remain calm and persevere to reach your goal.

You continue to move beyond the obstacles on this day's ride, and upon the last turn your car appears in the distance. You have just leaned something from this experience, perhaps wisdom. You overcame the physical challenge the environment presented. But more importantly, you conquered your own fear. That's accomplishment!

On many mountain bike rides in the wilderness, you will deal with fear, uncertainty, panic, greed, desperation. The best tactic is to go forward, think positively, and enjoy the excitement.

You need grit if you are going to enjoy remote mountain biking in the long run. Grit is the will power to survive—no matter what. Mentally, it means you must exhaust all possibilities and never, ever give up. If you break one leg, you hop. Two legs, you crawl. If you can't crawl, you tumble and squirm. But always believe you can make it. Always!

Using Your Instincts

Modern civilization dulls our sensory capabilities. In this super safety-oriented country, the so-called experts try to do our perceiving. They want us believing that their input is essential before we act upon anything. Morning, noon and night a media system warns and informs. Who needs it?

Anyway, when you transport yourself into the natural world, you will leave the bad news behind. When the distracting city noises give way to the sound of rushing water, chattering bogs and secluded forest, your senses come alive. If you choose to stay a few days or a week, you will definitely change your perspective on life. And that's the point.

Using your instincts is as simple as tuning in to what is happening around you. It's not an easy task, particularly if you are spreading your energies in too many areas. If you are rushing through your day, then you are probably out of touch with your senses.

Remote mountain biking can help you be in harmony with yourself. It puts you in touch with yourself and promotes a healthy life-style at the same time. It presents you with the opportunity to appreciate the message wilderness has to offer. And you will hear your inner-self more distinctly.

Making Decisions

Wilderness touring requires sound decisions. Good judgment and common sense are key attributes when you find yourself reaching the panic stage. It is nearly impossible to select the circumstance that would require critical decision-making *for you*. But everyone is different, so I will create several fictitious situations that might cause you to use your critical decision-making resources. I have had a number of close calls so you might as well benefit from my experiences.

The six steps I recommend when problems arise and you need to make a decision: **stop, think, check the maps, check the compass, check the odometer, and survey your present surroundings.** Conducted frequently, these steps can save you a lot of grief—and possibly your life.

Spend a moment calculating the distance you have traveled and the amount of time on your bike. Stop until you have formulated a solution. Thinking while pedaling distracts you from focusing on the solution and tends to cause additional errors. Finally, believe in your compass unless the sun tells you differently.

At this juncture you have several choices. You can turn back, stick with your plan or change the plan. Turning back means you would return the way you came—unless of course, you are more than halfway through a looping trail. The exception is when you definitely know the route, or you are close to an intersecting tar road (civilization). However, if you are unsure of your whereabouts—go back the way you came. Turn back at the first sign of these problems: serious bike trouble, sickness, injury, wet and cold conditions, loss of tools or supplies, dehydration, sleepy, uncharacteristically weak, sudden adverse weather, four hours before sunset, inoperative odometer. Or if you realize that you are unprepared physically, mentally or emotionally to continue.

The next option, sticking with your plan, means you would stick with your original plan and carry on. Stick with your plan when your body and mind are holding up well, supplies are adequate, there is no concern about getting lost, no bike troubles, no severe weather changes, your average speed is as predicted, and you have sufficient daylight to complete the trip.

The last option, altering the plan, means changing the original goal. That might be taking a different trail, staying out longer, etc. You might adjust your plans if you are lost, feel weak or disoriented, are severely sunburned, are low on supplies, have depleted your energy, notice threatening weather changes, are unhappy with the terrain, develop minor problems with your bike, experience slight physical problems, realize times and distances are out

84

of line with estimates, have a frightening encounter with an animal, encounter trail interference from logging operations, or other unexpected conditions.

The best method to avoid mistakes is to be aware, concentrate and exercise discipline. If you mess up, spend your energy rectifying the problem rather than worrying about it. Plan well, don't panic, and things will probably turn out just fine. When adversity strikes—strike back. Be confident and persevere.

Marking and Remembering Roads

You need to be somewhat of a detective when you are mountain biking—in that you need to pay attention to details. As you travel along your chosen trail, keep an eye out for unique physical features of the area. This includes scenes that stand out. If it is morning or afternoon, note the position of the sun and how it relates to sites. Next get off the bike at intersecting roads and take a compass heading. Take out your map and orient yourself to your location. As you move onward, look back and familiarize yourself with the crossing. That way you will better identify it upon your return. Look around as you ride and absorb details. Glance at the odometer and mentally note your energy level with the distance you have biked. Also, it's a good idea to know where you stand in relation to the overall run. Are there 10 miles to go or 15? Have I traveled half way yet? How long did it take me to get to this point? If you check, you will have the answers.

I have been bugging you throughout the book to mark intersections. This is *the* most important priority when remote mountain biking—for two reasons. One, so you don't get lost. Two, so you can relax.

There are a number of ways to mark your progress in the wilderness. Just be consistent. Before you learn, let's go over some trail designations. I classify them as:

Main Roads

Gravel-based and manageable by most cars and four-wheel drive vehicles. Some are gated, but most are not. Logging operations may be active. Very little or no plant growth in the center of the road. The surface is usually hard and has drainage. Some rocks may rest along side of the road. There are no felled, dead trees. Road is graded or maintained during non-winter months. Major snowmobile route.

Plant Roads

Gravel-based and partly to mostly manageable by four-wheel drive vehicles. Used during past logging operations but no present traffic. Plant growth is noticeable in the center of the road and is claiming ground on the sides. Often gated. The surface is ungraded and softer than main roads. Washed out drainage areas, bridges collapsed or missing, and metal culverts exposed. More rocks and possible dead tree vegetation, tire grooves, muddy areas, large puddles, etc., than the main roads. May be a snowmobile route.

Trails

Mixture of dirt, grass, mud, rocks. Some sections may be passable by four-wheel drive vehicles, but most are not. Plant growth abounds. Dead trees and brush are on the trail. Most trails spring from plant roads. Moose, deer and other animals use the trail frequently. There are natural drainage areas running in and across the trail. Almost never attempted by motorized vehicles. Streams may separate the trails. Some parts require walking the hike. Trails often used for snow mobiling only. Usually trail is easy to pick out, but it may break up in some areas.

Paths

No sections are passable by vehicle. Single track area is often engulfed by vegetation. Can be recognized as a path, but it often dead ends or splits off in other directions. It is an old trail grown in. Usually extremely wet and obstructed. Very dangerous and dark in remote country. May have to walk bike totally throughout path.

Marking Trails

Marking trails does take a bit of time, but the amount of time you would expend if you got lost, makes it worthwhile. My method for trail marking is simple. Use about five stones, if available, and pile them on the right side of the road, approximately 50 feet before reaching the intersection. In this way you can be positive of the direction from which you entered. Make sure the pile of rocks is well away from where vehicles pass but not covered in the brush.

This all sounds pretty easy, but there are potential problems, too. For example, if you do a lousy job of stacking the rocks, vibration from a passing logging truck could knock them down. Also be careful not to injure yourself when you create the marker. Look for stones that are lying around, never dig into the road.

Another way of marking is by memory. Sometimes you won't need to use stones if all the tributary roads are plant roads, trails or paths, and you are staying on the main road. In any case, it's best not to rely on recollection because it may be 12 hours before you return. Also it's difficult to predict the number of intersections on a route.

If only I could practice what I preach. In the past I have skipped marking, rationalizing that, "I will remember that intersection." But later in the afternoon when I am 40 miles down the road, it's a different story. It took a few near-death experiences to smarten me up. I trust you won't be as foolish.

Another Marking Tip

Carry a small stone in your right pocket to remind you which side of the road you are marking. It may sound unnecessary, but it won't be if you become disoriented or if there are piles of rock on both sides of the trail. Both situations have happened to me. To differentiate your rock pile from someone else's, include a couple of twigs with the rocks. Anyway, be creative and don't litter the landscape by using paper or surveyor's tape. A clump of grass or flowers will do fine. Pardon the repetition, but make sure your mark is consistent so you can relax and have fun.

Walking Your Bike

Walking is a part of almost every trek. Mountainous logging roads that cut through miles of high country will have you off your bike observing the country side at a slower pace. You are very likely to encounter many steep climbs on a day's journey. You could easily burnout trying to crank up all of them. But play it smart, conserve your energy and walk your bike when it's sensible.

When the grind is taxing and you are creeping along at only four or five mph, it's time to dismount. There is no reason to labor for an additional two mph. It's not worth the effort in the long run. You will need that vigor to complete the ride. Furthermore, you can walk three mph, while relieving overburdened pedaling muscles at the same time.

Walking has its own benefits. Depending on the road surface, it could be quieter, so you increase your chances of encountering wild animals. It's slower-paced so you notice more scenery than if you are flying past on a bike. Also, it improves your stamina. When you think about it, who wants to sit on the seat for eight or 10 straight hours anyway?

Pushing your bike is a good idea when you are touring isolated lands. It's good for your body. It's good for your mind. It's good for emotional balance.

How Not to Get Lost

There are a number of crude ways to locate your relative heading in the woods. You can use the trees, flowers, sun, general roadway direction, flowing water, landmarks, topographical elevation, approaching weather fronts and more, but the easiest way is to use a compass.

Be familiar with some basics before you take off on a ride. Study maps of the region you will be riding in. Make sure the charts go beyond your intended destination by at least 20 miles in every direction. This provides you with valuable options, especially if trouble arises. Take a small pencil with you—like the ones used for keeping golf scores. They are perfect because the graphite doesn't break easily and they are small enough to keep in your pocket.

When you leave the car, stop for an instant and check the sun's location. Remember it rises in the east, sets in the west, and moves south across the sky. Of course, the degree that it leans is determined by the season. For example, from December 20 to June 21, it works its way from southeast to southwest, taking a higher position every day until the last day of spring. On the first day of summer, its travel is the closest to true east at sunup and sunset. Then the process reverses as it heads back to the southern hemisphere again. Keep in mind that mountain-biking season in the north country extends approximately from ice-out (May 15) to mid-October. Therefore, the sun will be about a month shy of its highest potential at ice-out, and always be sinking deeper in the southern hemisphere after that. Anyway, by checking it before entering the woods, you will establish a directional reference point to use throughout the day.

Also, you can bring along a sunrise-sunset schedule. The New Hampshire Fish and Game Department distributes them as part of their hunting and fishing guide. Stop at any store that sells licenses to get one. Cut out the page, laminate it and slip it in your pack if you are not familiar with the area or feel more comfortable knowing the exact times.

If you make the ill-advised choice to travel without a compass, here are some nature tips to orient you. The sun is mostly in the southern hemisphere, so the north receives the least exposure during the day, which directly affects vegetation.

Branches are comparatively sparse on the northern side of trees. Yet, in order for this to be a guide, the tree has to be unobstructed from the sun by other trees, mountains, etc. If you keep an eye on the foliage or branch growth, you can roughly locate north. Moss grows on the north side of tree trunks. Be sure to use more than one specimen to make a decision. Survey many different trees in various locations to best establish north. Practice doing this and then compare the results with your compass. It might come in handy someday.

Flowers also provide hints. For example, in traveling east or west, you should notice more flowers on the north side of the road given the surrounding terrain is equally alike. Conversely, in traveling north or south, look for more flowers to be on the west side. Sometimes you can tell direction from how the trees and flowers bend too. Generally they grow toward the morning sun by leaning southeastward out over the road. Be careful, however, as various land features can influence growth and affect the direction they lean.

Landmarks such as mountains with projecting outcrops of rock, or those that have unique shapes can be a big help. Streams, rivers, lakes, ponds, bogs, open areas, certain types of trees, sand pits, boulders, fallen trees, bird nests and more will add to bearing recognition. The idea is to take mental notes of scenes, unique formations or oddities as you pass them.

Flowing water almost always leads to dams, bridges, roads and eventually to civilization. In general, people live in lowlands more often than highlands. Try following water downward if you are completely lost and can't find your way through the woods.

Climbing to elevations is another method to find your direction. Once you are up there, you may be able to piece the puzzle together from landmarks.

You will want to practice defining directions frequently. This book can get you started, but experience is your best guide. Try these methods along with a compass and your skills will improve with each ride. It took me years to feel comfortable with these techniques and I still I have a long way to go. Be smart—buy a compass and learn to use it.

Encountering Wildlife

I bet you're thinking it's about time I got to this part, right? Well, I've saved the best for last. Most of the time I prefer to ride quietly, keep my senses primed and cover territory. Because of this, I cross paths with plenty of living things.

If you want to encounter wild animals, you need to blend with the environment and be extremely alert. Traveling through the forest "on alert" can provide extraordinary opportunities. For example, a pungent smell could signal a moose or bear nearby. A shrill cry from a predator bird swooping from the sky could mean a rabbit or grouse is about to become dinner. A cracking branch may be a deer grazing nearby. The moving lump in the wavering field of grass in the distance is probably a coyote or fox.

When you pass over a wet or muddy area, stop and get off the seat to investigate. Lay your bike down softly rather than using the kick stand, because invariably the wind will send it crashing. Follow the footprints and don't step on twigs or kick any stones. Listen intently for sounds. If a deer suddenly appears, don't move an inch.

Most assuredly, the animal has already been alerted to your presence by its sixth sense. Here's where the discipline comes in. If the animal is motionless and staring directly at you, it's okay to return the stare. Enjoy the encounter instead of pulling out the binoculars or camera. You need to remain motionless while the creature checks out the situation.

Bugs, Bugs, Bugs

Yes, the bugs will bite, and the urge to scratch will be maddening. But don't break. In all likelihood, the deer will painstakingly nudge in your direction to get a better look. Remain immobile and you may see it exhibit a series of rituals that include foot-stomping, snorting, head bobbing, fake browsing, licking and twisting. It'll move closer until you blink or your scent causes it to high tail into the woods.

Encounters happen randomly in the North Country because there are many creatures and few people. Many creatures are nocturnal, but if you are out early in the morning, you will definitely run into some. Beaver, rabbit, coyote, fisher cat and raccoon, to name a few, may still be taking care of unfinished business sometimes as late as 9 a.m. Don't be surprised to see many of these creatures during the day, also.

Other signs reveal the presence of animals if you know what to look for. Moose walk the logging roads all the time, so if you see splashes of water near the prints, guess what? The beast probably just urinated or climbed out of a water hole. Fresh vegetation in the middle of the gravel means a rabbit is around. Of course, scat will not only tell the type of creature, but also what it was eating. Gnawed off bushes, scratched tree bark, exposed rotting logs, holes, hair and regurgitated food provide hints as well.

Respecting the environment of wild animals and "treading softly" has potentially great rewards. On the other hand, if you speed around making noise and abusing the land, you may be forfeiting some of the most precious resources we have. It could even be withdrawn from public use—remote mountain biking included. Please pedal softly and preserve this gift for future generations.

This bull moose is in the prime of his life. Well over 1,000 pounds in June. In October— 1,400 pounds!

Encountering Forest Logging Operations

Just because you will be biking in isolated country doesn't necessarily mean the passage ways you use will be isolated. If there is an active logging operation in the area, it may be quite busy. Tractor trailers, road-building equipment and dump trucks could all be working or traveling along these roads. The land is probably owned by a lumber company that builds and maintains the roads to extract timber. Don't get upset over the traffic. Because without lumber companies you wouldn't have the opportunity to enjoy remote mountain biking, fishing, hunting, snow mobiling or a myriad of other outdoor interests.

Be sure to always yield to these vehicles. They don't see many bikers and so won't be looking for you. When they come along— get off the road. Your life could depend on it.

What do you do when you find yourself unexpectedly on a logging route? First, estimate how much time you will be on it, then continue, turn back or change plans. If you continue and the trucks keep storming by, get off the route as soon as possible. It's no fun being "dusted."

If you stay on the road, here are some hints on how to negotiate the road with logging carriers. Ride on the right side of the gravel road (same as a car). The moment you hear or feel a truck coming, stop, pull yourself and your bike *off the road* and into the brush or woods. Wait until the truck passes. If you are not totally off the road, you risk getting hit. You will have enough time because the monstrous vehicles are tremendously noisy and vibrate the ground as they approach.

I rarely meet with truckers because I avoid the places where they are working. However, if I stumble upon an operation, I change plans and go in another direction. I've been known to return to my car and design a new route. It's not worth getting "dusti-sized" repeatedly.

When one of those machines, hauling a full load of trees lumbers around you, the things it kicks up are amazing and usually the dust storm takes more than a few minutes to clear. Once while I was journeying, a massive fire in a distant valley came into my view. I watched as the smoke billowed upward from the pine tops until it occurred to me that the smoke was just dirt powder. The dried muck was dislodged from a highballing transport and sucked into the sky by an updraft.

The dust cloud created by these large diesels makes it very difficult to breathe. The best advice is to keep your eyes down, mouth shut and turn away from the sand storm. Carry a small handkerchief in your T-shirt pocket just in case. You could even tie one around your neck—like a cowboy. Expect to experience similar situations every now and then, but take them in stride.

Give the Loggers Space—and Respect

Respect the loggers and their devotion to duty. They move at a fast pace along these roads to stay afloat in the tough wood and paper industry. We all need and use the products that they work to provide. We shouldn't take that for granted. I, for one, appreciate a good soft roll of Charmin, especially after a 50-mile ride.

One last suggestion about meeting up with active woodcutting operations—stay clear of machinery and don't bother the workers. Wait patiently from a distance until they allow you to continue, and then move right along. Exhibit your best manners, too. That means flashing a smile and a friendly wave of the hand. After you have cleared the work area, carry on and don't linger to watch. These guys are dropping, cutting and stacking giant trees, a job that's one of the most dangerous occupations in the country. Their hazardous work requires a great deal of concentration. Therefore, respect their space.

It appears to me that the logging industry is practicing in an environmentally sound manner. I have noticed that loggers leave plenty of cover around the watersheds, which are very sensitive environmental zones essential to wildlife populations. Some clear cutting does occur, too. In my opinion, this open land is good for the biodiversity of the area. After all, most of the thousands of square miles in northern New Hampshire and northern Maine are covered by thick forest. According to history, this same territory was used for farming a hundred years ago. Therefore, I believe that forest control is important. I think that logging operations have a long way to go before they interrupt the cycle of nature in this region of New England.

I have simply not seen any so-called "ugly sights" in my remote travels across this expanse. It doesn't matter whether I am biking through pine stands, hardwoods, fields, cutoffs, highlands or lowlands, everything is beautiful. My life has been tremendously enhanced by journeying through these secluded wilderness sections. My hat comes off to the generations of loggers who have made it possible.

Encountering Hunters

The remote north is probably less prone to hunting accidents than anywhere else in the state. People are more familiar with the woods and exercise good hunting practices in these parts, but that doesn't mean you should relax and willy-nilly push your bike through the brush.

During open rifle season for deer my recommendation is to discontinue off-road riding. During archery and muzzle loader season, pedal on a main road or plant road only. If you ride on trails or paths, you are asking for big trouble. Also, you should pick up a hunting guide by late summer so you will know the open-season dates and not fall off your bike when you hear gunfire.

I rarely mountain bike up north beyond the middle of October, nor in the south mid-November. However, I bike quite a bit in the early fall season during bear, deer, rabbit and bird season. Most people who hunt at this time are using a bow, one-shot muzzle loader or shotgun. Bear hunters use a guide, dogs or bait. Usually, this group of sportsmen is experienced and can be trusted to know their stuff. On the other hand, you may feel that going into the forest while hunters are present is too risky. I'm not giving up September and October, the prettiest two months of the year, just because hunting begins. We all ought to respect each other's activities.

The best way for bikers to live harmoniously with hunters is by pedaling quietly and wearing hunter orange clothing. That means refraining from talking loudly or making unnecessary noise. If you run across someone with a gun, make eye contact, slow down, or get off and walk your bike in order to show your cooperation. They will appreciate it and return the favor by being more tolerant of you. Furthermore, they will learn to recognize your sounds and sights which will help them to differentiate from other sounds and become safer hunters. Remember, many hunters have never seen bikers in the woods.

Don't panic if a shot rings out near you as you ride in the wilderness. Instead, stop! Try to locate the direction and source by scanning the area. If you don't see anyone, shout, "Hello! Biker over here. Is it okay to pass?" If you don't get an answer, repeat the message even louder. Be patient, sometimes people are target shooting, and will then walk toward their target (and hopefully away from you) after firing.

Gunfire is scary, but my experience indicates it does not occur often. However mistakes happen, and that is why you need to calmly consider whether you want to pedal during hunting season. If you choose to ride during hunting season, I reiterate my previous advice: Stay on the main roads or plant roads.

Encountering Anglers
You will encounter plenty of anglers as you roll along crossing bridges and bordering lakes. In a large sense, these people are going to be your comrades because mountain biking season corresponds with fishing season. They are going to be the ones who will be on isolated roadways. Birds of the same feather—fly together.

Many have been fishing since childhood and are good examples of experts without degrees. These types are stalwart adventurers in their own right.

Be sure you don't interrupt them and start gabbing about the fishing spots you may run across on your rides. There isn't anything more upsetting to adventurers than having others tell them about the special places that they have hunted months or years to locate. Pedal your bike in wild territories, keep secrets to yourself and let people make their own discoveries. In this way you will preserve the integrity of the region as well as the interests of individuals who have devoted their spirits to securing a rightful niche on water.

The Lodge

The lodge is where outdoor enthusiasts assemble—making it an integral part of the remote mountain biking experience. Late in the afternoon when people return from their outdoor adventures, they congregate to swap highlights and stories of the day's encounters. As you leave your vehicle and approach the building, you will hear laughter through its walls, where a large room is decorated with interesting wildlife and rock specimens from the area.

You will meet all kinds as you mosey around touching bear claws and moose racks or gazing at hummingbirds through the window. Coffee and home-cooked snacks tempt your palate. Here corporate executives, state legislators, mechanics, teachers, small business owners, lawyers, factory workers and retirees all speak the same language. It's a friendly site. You'll do more genuine socializing in this atmosphere than most others.

Conversation spans the gamut from ridiculous gossip to personal revelations about life. The place is unique. Here at night people rant, rave, swear and lie, but are not held accountable for it in the morning. The dwelling and outdoor environment fosters thinking about living for the moment. At dawn, all that was said the night before suddenly vanishes in anticipation of a new day's experience. Fishing, hiking, biking, bird watching, boating, canoeing or hunting is all that will matter until the sun retreats.

Visitors look similar in their lucky caps and grubby garb—until the talk begins. Self-proclaimed experts who normally fight for, hoard, and protect every ounce of information they have learned, suddenly open their chests of gold. Hard-earned wisdom is given freely. The generosity is overwhelming as people display their individuality, each with his/her own unique personalities. It's humanity at its best!

Old timers (60+) put the youngsters (40+) in their place, while those younger than 40, just listen, listen, if smart. Life stories are shared. Secret fishing holes, the 12-point bucks, raging rapids, salmon runs and jokes all have their turn. Short moments of quiet wrap around a lot of good old-fashioned bull. Backslapping, ribbing, roaring and glassy grins occasionally push someone (likely me) over the edge and we all end up howling in laughter. After everyone has sung their song, someone starts everyone else yawning. Then everyone heads for a bunk to dream of tomorrow's adventure.

There is a lodge such as this in Pittsburg, New Hampshire. It's a likely lodging destination as all the rides in this book begin in the Pittsburg area. The lodge is Spruce Cone Cabins and Campground. If you stay there, say "Hi" to Gary and Dot Bedell, the owners. You won't meet nicer people anywhere in the country.

Spruce Cone Cabins and Campground
U.S. Route 3   Box 13
Pittsburg, New Hampshire 03592
(603) 538-6361

STARTING POINTS

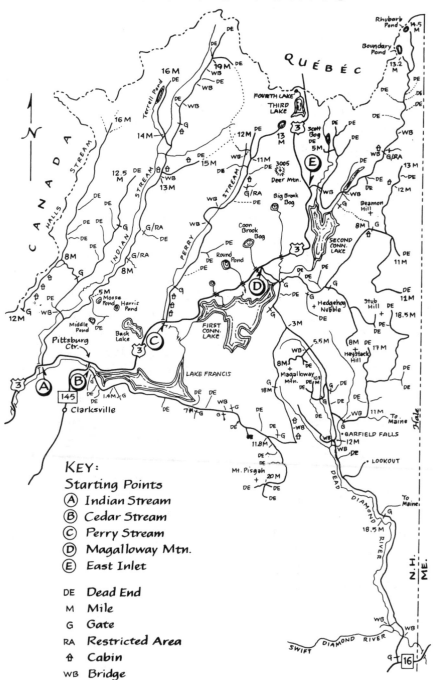

KEY:

Starting Points

Ⓐ Indian Stream
Ⓑ Cedar Stream
Ⓒ Perry Stream
Ⓓ Magalloway Mtn.
Ⓔ East Inlet

DE   Dead End
M   Mile
G   Gate
RA   Restricted Area
⚲   Cabin
WB   Bridge

CHAPTER 5

Maps and Route Notes

Getting to the Northern Territory

Getting to Pittsburg, NH, where all the rides begin, is easy. Here's how you do it. Take I-93 north to exit 35 and stay on Route 3 through Twin Mountain, Whitefield, Lancaster, Groveton, Stratford, North Stratford, Columbia, Colebrook, West Stewartstown to Pittsburg.

Once you reach Pittsburg, continue north on Route 3 for approximately five miles. You will see Spruce Cone Cabins and Campground. The Lodge and office are on your left. On your right are the pristine waters of Lake Francis.

Landmarks from Pittsburg Township Line
   (on Route 3 North) to East Inlet Road
   0.0 miles Connecticut River Bridge
   2.3 miles Tabor Road on left
   2.4 miles Logging yard on right
   * 2.6 miles Indian Stream Road (no road sign)
Starting point for Indian Stream and Hall Stream runs
   4.9 miles Fire Department, Police Department
   5.0 miles Post Office, general store, gas station, Pittsburg
      Center
   * 5.4 miles Store, gas station (Cross bridge into Clarksville

101

for **starting point for Cedar Stream runs.)**
6.5 miles Lake Francis launching area
7.0 miles Spruce Cone Cabins and Campground
* **8.0** miles Day Road—**starting point for Perry Stream runs**
8.5 miles Store, gas station, deli
9.7 miles NE Power—First Connecticut Lake Dam, Recreational Area
11.6 miles Round Pond Road (no road sign)
13.5 miles Moose Alley begins (this one-mile stretch of Route 3 is where moose are seen daily)
***14.5** miles Magalloway Mountain Road on right—**starting point for Magalloway runs**
14.5 miles Coon Brook Bog Road on left (no road signs, dirt road)
15.3 miles Big Brook Bog Road on left (no road signs, dirt road)
17.0 miles NE Power Dam (Second Connecticut Lake) Recreational Area
***21.1** miles East Inlet Road—**starting point for Boundary, Rhubarb Ponds and Scotts Bog runs**
* **Ride starting points. See map disclaimer on page 18.**

19 Routes from Pittsburg, NH

Each route is individually scaled for difficulty. Each also has an overall rating based on its relationship to the other 18, one being the easiest and 19 being the most difficult. Ratings are subjective.

The degree of difficulty rating system used in this book has five designations. All treks are in mountainous terrain.

Ride descriptions include the following:
(1) Length of trek
(2) Number and variability of ascents and/or descents (type of terrain)
(3) Physical quality of the road over the entire trek (sandy, loose gravel, clay, tire moguls, ruts, washouts, raised culverts)
(4) Obstacles (mud, water, rock, dead vegetation, bugs)

(5) Complexity of route (number of intersections)
(6) Total traveling time
(7) Propensity for adverse weather conditions

Spur Roads

Spur roads are short (usually not longer than three miles) deviations from the main route. In this book, they are not rated as part of any trek unless so designated on the map or in the route description section corresponding with each route. Each has its own separate degree of difficulty.

Ride Difficulty Rating System

1. Moderately easy. (Some off-road experience required.)

The terrain is accommodating, a few obstacles. Gradual climbs may include a couple of hills that grade steeply for a half mile or so. Ascents could be steady but are not very taxing. Roads are easily traversable with few if any challenges. Weather conditions probably will not have a major impact on the journey. Probably you will not have to walk your bike. Not very challenging.

2. Moderately difficult. (Considerable off-road experience required.)

The terrain is somewhat challenging. At least one steep climb extending a mile or so. There could be a number of half-mile climbs or moderate climbs that continue for miles. Road conditions are variable and include loose gravel, ruts, holes, tire moguls, protruding culverts and some dead vegetation. Weather conditions are more likely to impact the total traveling time and degree of difficulty. Some bike pushing may be required. Moderately challenging.

3. Difficult. (Rider must be very experienced at off-road biking.)

The terrain is generally steep with a few climbs extending beyond a mile. Moderate ascents are also challenging because of their length. Descents are particularly difficult as gravity combines with deteriorated road conditions and offers some rough riding. Mud, running water, dead vegetation, grass, puddles and marshy areas could be on the route. There could be a washed-out road or small stream to cross. Changes in weather conditions could significantly alter the degree of difficulty and traveling time. Complexity of the route requires excellent map-reading and compass skills. Physically and mentally challenging. Must push the bike at times.

4. Extremely difficult. (Expert experience required.)

The terrain includes many steep grades, some longer than two miles. Moderately steep climbs may continue upward for 10 miles. Road conditions include all possibilities. Ascents and descents are tremendously challenging and require upper and lower body strength. Standing and pedaling or frequently walking your bike is normal for this degree of difficulty. Weather changes could be a critical factor influencing total travel time and degree of difficulty.

+ A plus symbol means that the numerical rating is close to the next higher degree of difficulty. 1+ means that the route is close to a 2 rating but not quite as difficult.

Critter Encounters

The animals in this geographical location could be encountered on any of the 19 routes described. You are likely to see deer, moose, coyotes, bears, rabbits, fox, beaver, weasel, raccoon, fisher cats, otter, mink, bobcats, pine martens, squirrels, and porcupine, as well as other species.

Birds such as pileated woodpeckers, ruffed grouse, spruce grouse, ravens, owls, osprey, eagles, broad-winged hawks, herons, ruby-throated hummingbirds, goshawks, kingfishers, loons and many varieties of duck are common to the area, too.

Fact Sheet: 19 Northern NH Territory Rides

Scaled Ratings: A 1 rating is the easiest, 19 the most difficult.
Starting Points: All rides begin along Route 3 in Pittsburg, NH.
See specific start area with ride description below.
Degree of Difficulty: Description as noted on two previous pages.
Time: Estimated traveling time in hours to complete trip.
RT Miles: Round trip miles.

Ride No./ Start	Diffi- culty	Time	RT Miles	Scaled Rating	Ride Name
Map One:					
1 Indian Stream	2	4.5	24	7	Ind. Stream to Hall Stream—South
2 Indian Stream	2+	6.0	32	9	Ind. Stream to Hall Stream—North
3 Indian Stream	2	4.0	25	3	Ind. Stream—Western side
Map Two:					
4 Indian Stream	2+	6.0	42	5	Ind. Stream—Main Branch
5 Indian Stream	2	5.0	30	8	Ind. Stream—East Branch
6 Indian Stream	2	5.0	32	4	Ind. Stream—Terrell Pond
Map Three:					
7 Perry Stream	1+	3.5	24	2	Perry Stream—Main Branch
8 Perry Stream	2+	5.0	26	6	Perry Stream to Perry Pond
Map Four:					
9 Cedar Stream	4	8.0	43	16	Cedar Stream to Mount Pisgah
10 Cedar Stream	4+	10.0	50	18	Cedar Stream to Route 3
Map Five:					
11 East Inlet	1	3.0	15	1	East Inlet to Scotts Bog Area
12 East Inlet	3+	6.5	30	15	East Inlet to Bound./Rhubarb Pond
Map Six:					
13 Magal. Mt. Rd.	3	5.0	28	12	Mag. Mt. Rd. to Summit/Camp 5
14 Magal. Mt. Rd.	3	5.0	25	11	Mag. Mt. Rd. to Garfield Falls
Map Seven:					
15 Magal. Mt. Rd.	4	10.0	61	19	Mag. Mt. Rd. to Rt. 16 Wentworth
16 Magal. Mt. Rd.	3+	8.0	36	14	Mag. Mt. Rd. to Dead Diamond West
17 Magal. Mt. Rd.	4	8.0	41	17	Mag. Mt. Rd. to Diam. Ridge/Stub Hill
Map Eight:					
18 Magal. Mt. Rd.	3	5.0	23	13	Mag. Mt. Rd. to Stub Hill/Haystack Mt.
19 Magal. Mt. Rd.	2+	4.0	27	10	Mag. Mt. Rd. to Tin Camp Area

Ride 1: Indian Stream to Halls Stream—South

As you begin the Indian Stream ride, you roll through pasture land and past meandering streams. Horses and cows graze in the distant open country. As you pass by some camps, the road grades slowly upward for two miles with half a mile of steep ascent. Pileated woodpeckers flit across this section of stream. At mile three, turn left and cross a wood bridge over the stream. Bear right at the next intersection and travel steadily upward for over a mile. At mile five, take a left through an old open gate. Climb steeply for another mile and then enjoy an expanse of rolling ground. The road descends steeply after reaching the height of the land and converges at mile eight with Halls Stream Road. Take a left and continue about four miles to a gate on terrain that rolls peacefully toward Vermont. Look for bear scat and keep an eye out for bears, too.

Ride 2: Indian Stream to Halls Stream—North

Same as Ride 1 to mile eight (intersection of Halls Stream Road). Take a right on Halls Stream Road and travel north. The terrain winds upward and includes a number of steep climbs that are over half a mile long. At mile 11 and 13, you will pass a camp. Beyond this the trail begins to deteriorate for about two miles. At the dead end the road splits three ways. Each spur is grassy, boggy and rather undefinable. I don't recommend trying to push your way through these snowmobile trails. They all dead end for mountain bikes.

Views are good on the border of Vermont and New Hampshire. You see some beautiful timber stands mixed with a stream ecosystem. The return trip is easier as the downs overshadow the ups.

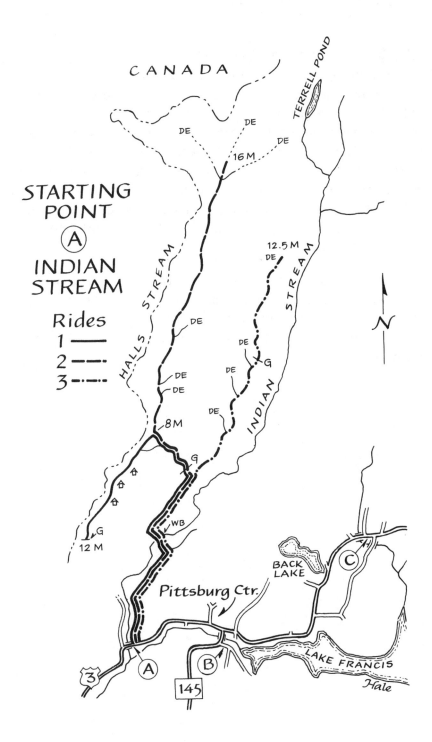

CANADA

TERRELL POND

DE
DE
DE
16 M
DE

STARTING
POINT
(A)
INDIAN
STREAM

HALLS STREAM

12.5 M
DE

Rides
1 ——
2 ———
3 —··—

N

DE
DE
DE
DE
G
DE
DE
DE
8 M
G

INDIAN STREAM

G
12 M
WB

BACK
LAKE

(C)

Pittsburg Ctr.

3
(A)
145
(B)
LAKE FRANCIS
Hale

Ride 3: Indian Stream—Western Side

This ride is the same as Ride 1 and 2 to mile 5. Continue past the five mile marker staying straight. There are some spur roads extending to the left and they are dead ends. The terrain generally climbs in a moderate fashion but does so in a roller coaster manner. It's somewhat taxing. Be aware that the gravel is loose in some spots and there is almost no shade on this run. In the hot sun, this route is significantly more intense. At mile 9 there is a gated road that you can pass through. Continue onward until the road dead ends. There is only one section of road where the stream is in view.

This route is a great training route for getting accustomed to remote mountain biking because it has some moderate and gradual climbs as well as a couple of short, steep stretches. Mountains break up the ride to keep it interesting and the country is open—providing good views.

Ride 4: Indian Stream—Main Branch

This ride is the same as Ride 1, 2 and 3 to the three-mile marker. Travel three miles to the intersection of Indian Stream and go straight. At 3.7 miles look to the right for a moose wallow and marsh. In early summer (if the marsh is full) moose love to play in the water while they tear vegetation from its bottom. Beavers are also prevalent in this hearty wetland environment. It's imperative that you bear left at each major intersection of road, always staying near the stream. You will pass along the stream in many sections so if you want to swim—have fun.

The terrain generally ascends gradually and includes some short, steep climbs and descents. Deer are all over the place. Camps intersperse the trail throughout the ride. Expect to cross three or four wooden bridges before you dead end over 20 miles in. This route is a great training ground for higher-level remote mountain biking. On a Sunday it is particularly quiet and serene because few people are on it.

Caution: Indian Stream connects with Perry Stream. The passageway is confusing, marshy, undefinable and dangerous. I don't recommend trying to navigate this area, and it's not included as part of this run.

Ride 5: Indian Stream—East Branch

This ride is the same as Ride 4 to 13-mile marker or Depot Camp. At 13 miles, where there are camps on both sides of the road, you will see a spur road to the right. This is East Branch Road or Ridge Runner Road. It ascends steeply for over a mile and then levels out to some pretty open country. Bears frequent this area, so stay tuned in. You will pass an old camp on the left side of Ridge Runner Road. Again, this road connects to Perry Stream but is for snowmobiles only. It's dangerous to attempt this connection as the road becomes overgrown, marshy and undefined. It is not included as part of this run.

This route is good training for higher-level remote mountain bike rides because it has a little of everything: steep, moderate

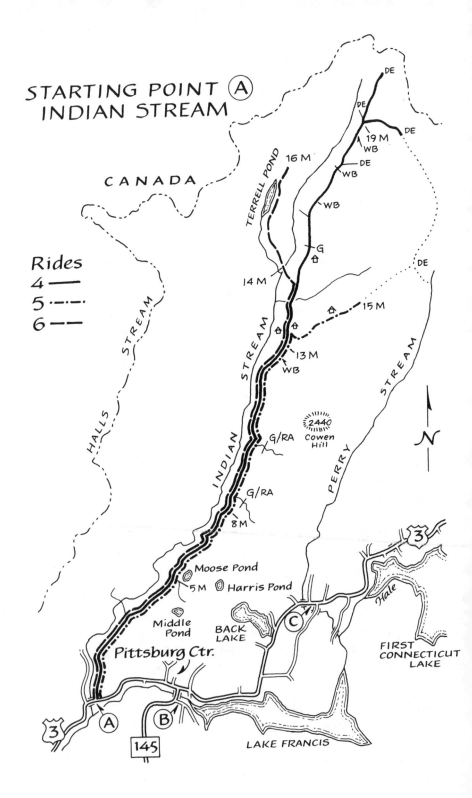

STARTING POINT Ⓐ
INDIAN STREAM

CANADA

Rides
4 ——
5 ·—·—·
6 ——

TERRELL POND

DE

DE
DE

19 M
WB

16 M

DE
WB

WB

G
⌂

14 M

DE

15 M
⌂

STREAM

13 M
WB

⌂
⌂

2440
Cowen
Hill

STREAM

G/RA

PERRY

STREAM

N

INDIAN

G/RA

HALLS

8 M

Moose Pond

5 M Harris Pond

Middle
Pond

BACK
LAKE

Ⓒ

Hale

FIRST
CONNECTICUT
LAKE

Pittsburg Ctr.

3

3

Ⓐ

Ⓑ

145

LAKE FRANCIS

and rolling terrain. Mountains on all sides keep the scenery interesting.

Ride 6: Indian Stream—Terrell Dam Road

This ride is the same as Ride 5 to mile 14. At approximately mile 14, look for a road to the left. It may be marked with a sign: West Branch Dam. Take this left and travel over a culvert bridge into a marshy area where you will be refreshed by the sound of gurgling water and smallfry trout jumping as you pass. The road continues for a few miles along Terrell Dam and Bog. The area is backdropped by mountains. It's a panoramic view where the blue stands out against a sea of green. Pedal until the road dead ends, and enjoy the scenery again on your return trip.

This is a great training route for higher-level remote mountain bike rides.

Ride 7: Perry Stream

As you progress down Day Road or Perry Stream Road (it's referred to by both) stay left at intersections, always following the stream northward. There are many spur roads to the right throughout the trip, so be careful to keep with the stream. Mile markers are posted on this road but may not be accurate. The terrain rolls generally upward for the first seven miles and then climbs moderately to mile 12. There are no real steep ascents beyond a half mile, making the journey pleasing and nontaxing, too, by remote wilderness standards, that is. The route crosses over the stream in two places and there are camps interspersed throughout the run. The last mile is somewhat grassy and muddy before the road dead ends.

The return trip is a breeze as the descents outnumber the climbs. Many deer occupy this area, where mountains provide a stunning backdrop. If you want to investigate spur roads, be aware that they are steep in most instances and could significantly drain your energy.

This is a great route to begin your quest for higher-level remote mountain bike rides.

Ride 8: Perry Stream to Perry Pond

This ride is the same as Ride 7 to mile 10.8. When you hit mile 10.8, look to the right for a 4-wheel drive road. This is the passageway to Perry Pond. The road to the pond is steep, muddy, rocky, grassy and has a ton of bugs—and some running water, too. You may have to walk your bike part of the way.

Perry Pond is the ultimate in seclusion, having only one camp that I am told has been owned once by a previous New Hampshire senator and once by a New Hampshire governor, too. It features prairie grass around the edges, mountains as a backdrop, and pine forest surrounding it. If you choose to bike the forest path, walk over the spillover dam to enter. The path has you strolling under beautiful pines and over a mixture of fantastic fern and clover. The clover creates a blanket of green. The abundance of clover creates a unique spectacle to experience. Do not get close to the camp. Respect privacy rights. Be careful on the challenging descent. Enjoy the last mile of the run to Perry Stream Road.

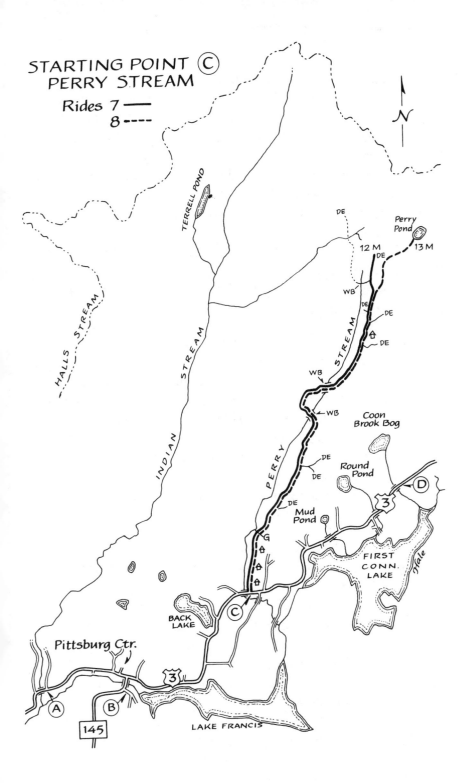

STARTING POINT Ⓒ
PERRY STREAM
Rides 7 ——
8 - - - -

N

TERRELL POND

DE

Perry
Pond

12 M
DE   13 M

HALLS STREAM

INDIAN STREAM

STREAM

WB

DE

DE

WB

WB

Coon
Brook Bog

PERRY

DE

DE

Round
Pond

Ⓓ

3

DE

Mud
Pond

FIRST
CONN.
LAKE

G

BACK
LAKE

Ⓒ

Pittsburg Ctr.

3

Ⓐ

Ⓑ

145

LAKE FRANCIS

Ride 9: Cedar Stream to Mount Pisgah

Cedar Stream Road follows along Lake Francis for seven miles and generally roller coasters for that distance. Bear left at .2 mile and again at 1.4 miles. Travel over a wooden bridge and avoid two spur roads at 1.6 and 1.8 miles on the right. Ride until you come to a ranger station at 3.5 miles. Bear left there and continue past a right spur at 4.8 miles and one on the left at 7.0 miles. Pass by another gated road at 7.3 miles on your right and go through a gate and over a wooden bridge at 7.4 miles. At 8.9 miles bear left and pass over another wooden bridge at 9.0 miles. Shortly beyond this point you will pass by a gated road to the left and at 10.1 miles, a spur to the right. All the while you will be pedaling harder as the road steadily climbs.

At 10.6 miles a great view of Lake Francis appears and closes just as fast. So stop and enjoy it. You are on top of Roundtop Mountain. Pass by a spur road to the right at 11.0 miles and one at 11.7 on the left. At 11.8 miles, bear right on the gravel and follow this road all the way up to Mount Pisgah, about eight more miles. During the stretch, avoid spur roads and cross one last wooden bridge before you climb steeply to the height of the land. At the end of the road, it'll split three ways into the backside of the mountain. This creates a tremendously beautiful backdrop. In the fall, it is glorious to encounter.

Ride 10: Cedar Stream to Route 3

This ride is the same as Ride 9 as far as Mount Pisgah Cutoff Road at 11.8 miles. Bear left at the Mount Pisgah Cutoff and descend another mile. Pass by a spur road to the left that is gated. Then the gravel rises moderately for another mile where a camp is on the right and a spur road on the left. The road rolls downward again for over a mile. Here on the back of Magalloway Mountain, wildflowers and butterflies flourish. A short distance beyond this, you will pass between two camps and then begin a long hard, steep ascent that goes for nearly two miles. At about mile 18, you will come to another gate where you will bear left. The terrain continues upward but more gradually and in a rolling pattern. You will pass by one spur on the right before you reach

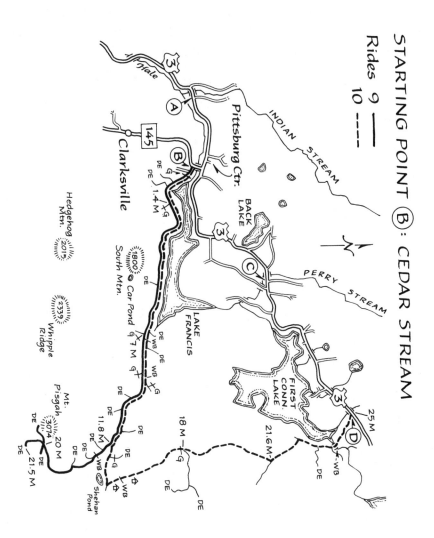

STARTING POINT Ⓑ : CEDAR STREAM

Rides 9 ——
10 ---

115

Magalloway Mountain Road. Take a left and cruise down to the Connecticut River and 1.2 miles beyond for Route 3. If you can't make the return trip, follow Route 3 southward for about 12 miles to Pittsburg Center. The return trip through the woods is tough but is easier than the first half of the journey. It'll be very taxing and a hell of a grind.

This is definitely an iron-man route. That aside, it is a route that will carry you through superb wilderness without being isolated in a locked-gate area.

Ride 11: East Inlet to Scotts Bay Area

Begin at East Inlet Road. Just after you cross the wooden bridge over the Connecticut River, bear left. Follow this road straight to Scotts Bog. A few spur roads appear on your right— they all dead end. Investigate every inch of these roads so you can get a basic idea of the terrain. Scotts Bog harbors abundant wildlife, and is a spectacular mountain marsh with great diversity. You may have to get off your bike and peek through small sections of trees to see the bog in some areas. It's worth getting off your bike to see all the wildlife.

This is a great place to take pictures of the serene wilderness, too. If you have the energy left when you return to the river, go straight and take a look at the inlet water environment. Traveling a couple of miles up the inlet brings you to a water fowl management area on your left. Welcome to remote mountain biking.

Ride 12: East Inlet to Boundary Pond and Rhubarb Pond

When you cross over the Connecticut River bridge, take a right and begin your journey up East Inlet Road. After 1.3 miles and your first moderate climb, you will see a gated road to the right. Pass by this road continuing on Inlet Road for the next few miles. At 4.0 and 4.1 miles avoid spur roads to the right. At 6.4 miles a spur road to the right appears and has two boulders next to it. Don't take it.

Cross a wooden bridge here and check for a camp on the left, and a sand pit to your right. Travel another mile and cross over another wooden bridge. At 8.1 miles a spur road begins to your left, but avoid it, as you climb steeply for over a mile. Views begin to appear as the territory opens somewhat. Continue on Inlet Road and do not take any spurs that appear at 10.3 miles to the left and 10.4 miles to the right and 10.8 miles to your right. Panoramic views now unfold before you. Pass by a road to the left at 11.2 miles and look for a superb mountain marsh at 11.5 miles. At one time two dead bull moose were found in this bog, horns locked together.

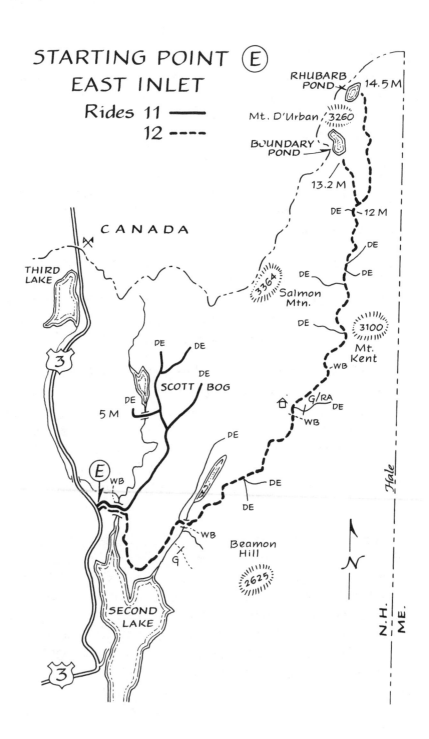

STARTING POINT Ⓔ
EAST INLET
Rides 11 ——
12 ----

RHUBARB POND ✕ 14.5 M

Mt. D'Urban 3260

BOUNDARY POND

13.2 M

DE 12 M

CANADA

DE

DE

DE

3364
Salmon Mtn.

DE

DE

3100
Mt. Kent

WB

DE DE

DE

SCOTT BOG

DE

DE

5 M

G/RA DE

WB

DE

Ⓔ WB

DE

DE

WB

Beamon Hill

2625

G

THIRD LAKE

3

SECOND LAKE

3

Hale

N.H. ME.

N

At 12.1 miles you travel through a swampy area over the road. At 12.4 miles, Boundary Pond Road heads to the left. About a mile steeply upward, the road ends in a parking area. It's a short .2 mile hike to the pond. Walk your bike here. Go back to the intersection and take a left and descend a half mile and then climb steeply for over a mile to reach Rhubarb Pond. Both ponds are pristine examples of an isolated mountain ecosystem. Your first visit to these wilderness areas may well help you to understand the true meaning of awesome.

You must be in great condition to take this journey.

Ride13: Magalloway Mountain Road to Summit and Camp 5 Area

The road delves from Route 3 into the wilderness, quickly passing over the Connecticut River between First and Second Lake. Go straight after the river and soon (1.8 miles) a spur to the left appears. Continue past this, bearing left at the next two intersections. "Tower" may be nailed to a tree pointing you to the left. The climb becomes steep for the next 2.5 miles, leveling out at mile 5. Here, the land begins to slope in your favor and at 5.5 miles the summit road is on your right.

The passageway upward is approximately three miles but is not as bad as it may appear from Magalloway Mountain Road. Anyway, a hiking trail (one mile) must be walked from the end of the road in order to reach a fire tower. Magalloway Mountain is the second highest peak in the area. Stub Hill is highest. From the tower you can see Maine, New Hampshire, Vermont and Canada. The views are outstanding. I do not recommend taking your bike up the trail. It is steep and quite dangerous. You can explore the mountain summit for additional fun.

Upon descending the mountain, return to Magalloway Mountain Road and turn right. Travel mostly down for three miles to an intersection on the right. During this three mile stretch you will experience the dramatic effect of being in the backdrop of this majestic peak.

At 8.5 miles, take a right and pass by a camp on your left and then pass through a gate and over a bridge. Bear right at the first intersection and when the road splits investigate both spurs until they dead end. Here you will experience total solitude while surrounded by old-growth pine stands. Keep an eye out for the elusive Pine Martin. Return by the same route being careful about your direction. A wrong turn could have you traveling south into a maze.

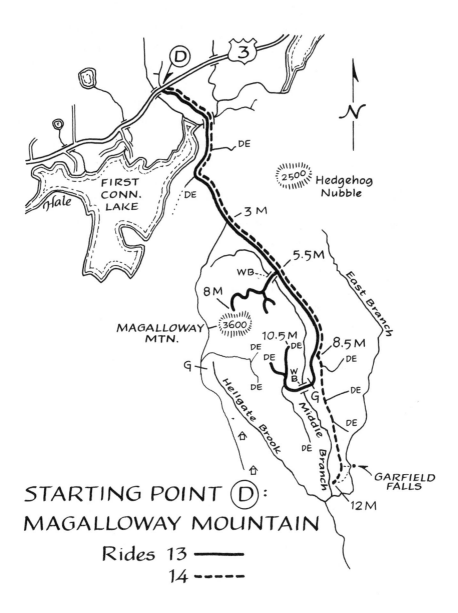

STARTING POINT Ⓓ:
MAGALLOWAY MOUNTAIN
Rides 13 ——
14 -----

Ride 14: Magalloway Mountain Road to Garfield Falls

This ride is the same as Ride 13 to mile 8.5 on Magalloway Mountain Road. Instead of turning right off Magalloway Mountain Road toward Camp 5, go straight on Magalloway Mountain Road. You will be traveling south. At approximately mile 9 you will see a spur road to the left with a gate on it. This road goes two miles to dead end and has nice views but do not take it for this ride unless you have enough energy to do so. A quarter mile farther you will see another left that dead ends at the river. Continue right for another mile or so until you see a gated road to the left. This road crosses the East Branch of the Dead Diamond River and will be explored on Ride 17. Anyway, stay right, pass by a camp on the right and continue to mile 12 where the road widens into a parking area. This is where you must hike in the woods about a half mile to see the falls. The trail is marked but do not bring your bike down it.

Garfield Falls is one of the most serene and isolated river falls in New England. Enjoy. Return the way you came.

Ride 15: Magalloway Mountain Road to Route 16— Wentworth Location

This ride is the same as Ride 14 as far as Garfield Falls. At Garfield Falls take the four-wheel-drive road to the right and travel beyond some boulders, through muck, puddles, dead vegetation and washed-out road for a couple of miles before the road dries out. You will pass by a couple of spurs to the left. Stay on your course southward until the road ends at an intersection. I call this the "snowmobile intersection" because a wooden sign may be still posted there. If it is not, mark your road and bear left eventually crossing a wooden bridge. The river runs over some nice ledge here and it's a great place to rest or investigate. Continue southward as the road winds its way through the valley. A few miles down the road you will see a wooden bridge crossing the river. Stay straight and do not cross the river. The next spur on your left leads to what I named Mountain Bike Steve Lookout. It's a short climb that will allow you to view the whole Dead Diamond River valley and mountains to the north. Go back to the main road, take a left and continue until you reach a gate. Don't take the road to the left or you will end up in Maine. Go through the gate and travel gently for the next nine miles where you will see a ranger station on the right. Go straight here for another mile to a bridge where the Dead Diamond River meets the Magalloway River. This site is the home of nesting ospreys. Do not disturb them—keep moving. Another mile or so and you will reach another gate and then Route 16. Return the way you came and be careful not to pass by the snowmobile intersection because a short distance beyond is another identical looking intersection.

Enjoy the best of remote mountain biking on this route. The trek back to your vehicle will be more strenuous so save some energy for it.

Ride 16: Magalloway Mountain Road to Dead Diamond— West

This ride is the same as Ride 15 as far as the snowmobile intersection. When you reach the snowmobile intersection, take a right and travel a short distance to a wooden bridge. You will

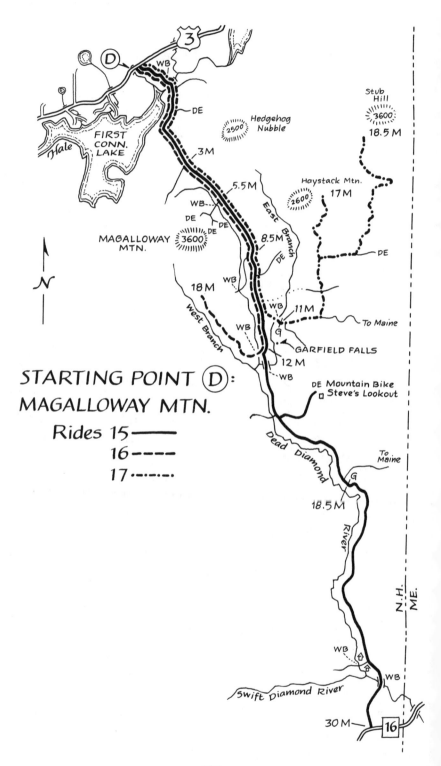

STARTING POINT ⒟:
MAGALLOWAY MTN.
Rides 15 ———
16 - - - -
17 ·—·—·

cross the main branch of the Dead Diamond River and then come to an intersection. Bear left and follow this road a few miles to a dead end. This road features wide open views of a spectacular valley. In the summer, you will see fields of yellow flowers. Quite a sight.

Keep an eye out for bears eating raspberries during August. Upon your return, make sure you take the snowmobile intersection instead of the one before it because they look very similar. The trek back to Route 3 is more strenuous so prepare yourself for it.

Ride 17: Magalloway Mountain Road to Diamond Ridge and Stub Hill

This ride is the same as Ride 14 as far as east branch of the Dead Diamond River. If you check out the Ride 14 notes you will recognize that at 10.5-11 miles down Magalloway Mountain Road from Route 3, you passed by a gated road to your left. This road crosses the river—East Branch. Travel through the gate, heading east (upward) for a mile. Then take a left. This road winds northward. Pass through a four-way intersection until you come to a spur road to the right. Turn right here and pedal upward in an easterly direction to where the road splits to the right. Go straight, traveling northward and steeply upward for over two miles to dead end on the backside of Stub Hill. The views unfolding here are spectacular and feature the best of remote mountain biking. It's bear country. Big bear country!

Be careful returning—where the road splits it's very steep. At the next intersection take a left and discover open-cutoff country where moose frequent. It's only about 1.5 miles of road. Return to the point where you initially took your first spur, and if you are up to it, take a right for two miles and discover the beauty of Haystack Mountain's backside. This is where I bushwhacked through the woods in one of my stories. (Check out the essays in the back of the book.) You are in the midst of Diamond Ridge so I wouldn't recommend trying it because the forest is like a jungle in there and you can easily become disoriented.

On your return, if you turn right at the four-way intersection, you will come out at the river where the bridge is out. Cross the river (if it's safe to do so) and you will be on Magalloway Mountain Road about 9.5 miles from Route 3. It's a short cut but only if you feel capable of trying it. Until you are real familiar with the territory, you're better off sticking to the route outlined here.

This journey includes the best of mountain backdrop scenery.

Ride 18: Magalloway Mountain Road to Stub Hill and Haystack Mountain

Begin at Route 3 for 1.2 miles. When you cross the bridge over the Connecticut River, take a left. This is Smith Brook Road. At about 2.3 miles you will come to a spur road to your left, and at 2.8 miles a gated road to your right. Both spurs dead end. At 3.5 miles two more spurs intersect from the left and they dead end too. Travel between four camps to the next gate on the right. Passing through the gate and continuing 1.5 miles upward, you will come to another intersection on the left. This road goes up Stub Hill and dead ends shy of the summit. You will have to hike up if you want to go all the way.

It is said that there is a bottle on the top with the names of all who dared make the climb. I don't recommend it, but it's up to you. The views of the Connecticut Lakes and of Maine are tremendous. There is a pond at approximately 3,000 feet. It's about a 20-minute hike from the logging road. But again, it's difficult to find, so I wouldn't recommend it. Returning to the place where you took a left to Stub Hill, go left about a mile to the last intersection on this run. Bear right and you will climb 1.5 miles steeply upward to Haystack Mountain. The road dead ends short of the summit but it is easy to walk up the skidder trails created by logging operations. Don't take your bike. Hike through dead vegetation and raspberry bushes to reach the summit, if you choose to make the climb. The views are spectacular and include almost all of Pittsburg, NH, some of Maine, Canada and maybe even Vermont. Be careful on the descent—gravity really pulls you on this one. This area offers the best panoramic wilderness views imaginable.

Ride 19: Magalloway Mountain Road to Tin Camp Area

This ride is the same as Ride 18 to the second gate. When you reach the second gate on Smith Brook Road, go straight past it for four miles to a tin-roofed camp ("Tin Camp"). Turn right and pass through the gate and travel upward. Do not take the spur road to your left. Instead stay straight until the road descends and eventually splits. Investigate both roads until they dead-end.

You will see tremendous open country here because timber has been cut. It's bear country too, and you will probably see piles of bear scat on the road. There is something very appealing about this terrain as you will experience. I won't spoil it by telling you any more.

STARTING POINT Ⓓ : MAGALLOWAY MTN.

Rides 18 ———
19 ----

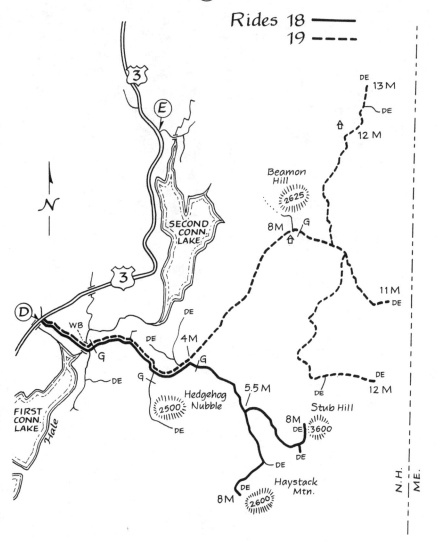

Follow me for adventures and thoughts with Mountain Bike Steve.

CHAPTER 6

Adventures and Thoughts

Introduction

Years ago, Easterners who got bogged down, bored and altogether fed up with their lot, packed up and moved west. Today when we feel the same way, the compass needle should point north to northern New Hampshire.

Come with me, forget your problems and experience the moment. But first let me tell you who I am and how I came to be Mountain Bike Steve.

Several years ago I was out on my one-speed bike adventuring in the southern tier of New Hampshire. I had been off-road for 10 hours, traveled about 70 miles and was just breaking out of the woods onto tar road when it happened.

Four little kids, two girls, two boys, came running toward me. "Moose, moose!" they exclaimed. I looked around, saw nothing and rolled forward. I was wet, beaten, mean and hungry and all I wanted to do was get to my car about two miles up the road. But because I love kids, I was compelled to turn around. As I did, there he was, a big bull moose standing in the road behind me.

Now the "Fabulous Four" began chasing the thing into a wet area near a pond. It was October. The moose was in a rut and could have been dangerous. So I hurried into the woods, pedaling through giant puddles to meet the "Fearless Four." "That animal is mean this time of year," I told them. "Let's get out of here. Now!"

The "Fearless Four" became the "Frantic Four." With eyes swelled and legs pumping, they retreated toward the tar road. These youngsters meant business as they ran with reckless abandon through the middle of giant puddles. One little blonde girl about 4 or 5 years old, was up over her knees in water when she took a fall head first into the brown muck. She never stopped. She bounced up, eyes still bulging and little legs pumping like a locomotive. The muck was all over her, as if she had taken a pie in the face. It was funny as hell.

The drenched kids made it out. "Go home now and change up," I warned, and they ran off. I know, you're saying, "Get to the point." Here it is.

One year later, as I was coming out of the woods at exactly the same spot, a youngster was sitting on his bike in the road watching me. As I passed by, I heard, "Hey mister, aren't you the guy who saved us from the moose?"

Now I was in heaven. I said, "Yeah."

He looked me squarely in the eye, with total seriousness. "What's your name anyway?" Well, I had all I could do to keep from saying "the Lone Ranger." But I said, "Mountain Bike Steve, the only one-speed biker in the world." You should have seen his face. It lit up like his daddy just brought him home some candy. I was happier than he was over the whole thing, but I played the game.

This story should help you to understand the kind of guy I am. I'm just an ordinary man who lives in the southern rat race section of the state. This means that every few months the stress levels add up. My wife and I agree that it's almost always work that causes my stress, but occasionally my home life is a factor.

In any case, when it happens I make like an Easterner of yesteryear and head out. The only difference is that instead of moving west, I go north into northern New Hampshire and Maine. I take my one-speed mountain bike with me.

Actually, the very instant I make the decision to get away, my stress begins to lessen. Planning takes about a week for me. First, I make a list. This takes about three days because I'm so burnt-out and excited at the same time that I can't think or remember where I hid the list from my previous trip. When that's done, I pack. I'm going alone. And if I forget something, I won't be able to blame my wife. (Just kidding— I couldn't resist.) Finally, I pack the car the night before and turn in.

If things go normally, I wake up at 1 a.m. and watch the clock until 6 a.m. Soon I'm heading up I-93 in a daze. On the way up I'm reliving the smell of the pine trees, the feel of the wind, the cool air on my face, the quiet around me, and most of all, the animal encounters. All the while my energy level picks up in anticipation.

I rent a room in a cabin or motel, dump my gear and change into my gritty mountain bike clothes. Next, I put my lucky silver coins in my pocket and slap on my lucky cap that has never been washed, unless you count the soakings it has taken in the rain and swamp water. Finally I'm off and into the woods.

The Flight of the Butterflies

Night has fallen upon the isolated cabin in Pittsburg, New Hampshire. No television blares—only silence permeates the room. Occasionally a vehicle passes on the road below. The door and windows are open. A screened-in porch echoes with the crickets and frogs who unite in a chorus of song. They help me recount my adventures of the last three days. Come along.

The day is cool, dry, and the sun is out full time. I've parked the car off Route 110, just east of Groveton, NH. I'm rolling up the road toward Nash Stream. After a couple of miles passing gurgling streams, the tar turns to dirt. And I'm smiling.

When you're in the North Country, the first thing you notice is the smell. In fact, I am lavishing in it. I take deep breaths, filling my nostrils. There's nothing like it. The combination of mud, evergreen trees, freshly cut wood, and rotting wood permeates the air. It's so good I have to look down to see if I'm pedaling. This is my first visit ever to Nash Stream. My mind therefore, is transfixed in the present. Newness is the best therapy in life.

My first visual encounter comes from the standout wildflowers along the road side. In the north they grow to full size. In fact, when the plants are in bloom up here, biking is transformed into scene after scene of pure paradise.

Sometimes when the road never seems to quit rising and the burden of traveling up gets really heavy, it's these flowers that keep me going. I call it energy at no cost. That's the deal from nature. All you have to do is forget the past and stop worrying about the future. Just experience the moment and fill your tank.

Today I'll travel a 40-mile trip that includes the Trio Ponds area. I have two quarts of water and three packages of peanut butter crackers. Yet what's important, is that I have my spirit. I'm not alone. But it's the here and now that matters.

Yellow and Black Tiger Swallowtail Butterflies escort you through the woods mid-June through early July.

I must rise to meet the harmony of this world, for I am just another creature out here. One that is accepted without condition, no better and no worse. Therefore I will draw more from nature than food or water.

Yellow and black tiger swallowtail butterflies are everywhere. They are the same size and shape as monarchs but much brighter in the sun's reflection. As I stand and pedal upward, they seem to come toward me forever. I'm in a state of wonder because of it. Maybe they zone in on a direction.

Bang! I'm hit square in my eyes. But it just bounces off and heads south. Each time I find myself questioning why—bang!—another hits me. The message comes through loud and clear. Don't think, experience it now. There is never an instant during the day that I am without their company.

Trudging ahead, I anticipate that upon my return, the glorious butterflies will ride with me, and they do. These creatures fly down the road looking for mates and congregate in great numbers on animal scat.

They'll fly approximately eight to 12 miles an hour and at about four or five feet above the ground. So as I cruise along one will be at eye level for a hundred feet at a time. Then it will see a mate and break away. But another picks up, and this goes on all day. There are no words to adequately describe the experience.

Do you know what it feels like to float with the butterflies? I can see into their eyes. I can see the hidden colors of the rainbow scattered about their tails. Together we move along through pockets of heat. A calmness surrounds us. We're enveloped by the heady scent of pine. It's total freedom in every sense of the word. Everything works together. Nothing is the same. And I've been accepted.

At one point during the day, I creep my bike forward on almost-level ground when suddenly a partridge blasts out from the brush and passes inordinately close to me. It does not fly far. As I pass without stopping, I hear it squealing and making noise in the bushes. After the experience, it occurs to me that the bird came close because she was protecting her little ones. The squealing is an injured bird call designed to attract predators toward the feigning bird and away from her newborns.

Once again, later in the day, a partridge jumps out at me. This time I stop and approach the direction from which I am accosted. Sure enough, the hen goes into its distress call. She also storms around with her head down and tail up to get me close to her. I refrain. Then I search for her clutch, which I find scrambling in the long grass.

The hatchlings look like little brown puffballs the size of baby chickens. They're hopping all over the place. It's great, but I'm not staying long because the mother bird is rattled. It's getting late anyway, and there's a lot of road ahead. I pedal on, because soon another day in the northern regions of New Hampshire will draw to a close.

Where the Moose Roam

The day is cloudy. But every once in a while the sun shows. The air is cool and a light breeze rustles in the leaves. I park the car just off Route 3 on East Inlet Road in Pittsburg. The ride I'm taking starts on dirt, and that's good. I like to ride on dirt. This is new territory for me and that makes it doubly good. I want my mind in the present.

After checking my maps I float downhill and enter into the big country. At the first intersection I have to decide. I go left thinking it's East Inlet Road. When you are biking up in these parts, you're never quite sure about where you are unless you know the area. New roads are going in all the time, and maps are always outdated. For me, this just adds to the excitement.

Not more than 10 minutes into the trip I encounter the first creature. A very large brown hare is sitting next to a road gate chomping on something green. My movement startles it and off it goes, taking a foot of vegetation along. Slowly I roll to the area where the hare disappeared, but there is no sign. The encounter has heightened my energy level; my senses are keen as the adventure continues.

Four or five miles up the road, I see Scott's Bog through the trees. At this point, I realize the first left I took was a wrong turn, but who cares? Eventually the road ends in a cul-de-sac covered with mud and rotting wood. It's amazing how these dead ends all look and smell the same. Logging machines need room to turn so that's what creates the cul-de-sac. Since the road is ending, there's no need for them to clean up. The aroma, therefore, is intense.

Today I want to reach Boundary Pond before the day is done. The sky looks threatening at times, and it bothers me. Boundary Pond, on the border shared with Quebec, is about as far north as New Hampshire goes. But to reach it, I have to return to the intersection where I made the wrong turn. After a brief peek at Scott's Bog, I return to that intersection, where my speedometer hits 10 miles.

Red fox are instinctively keen creatures. Most of the time they're watching us—but we may never know it.

From here I estimate the trip to be about 15 miles north, so there's no time to waste. I hate to rush and that is why I'm uncomfortable. There is this sense of uncertainty because of the weather. I listen to these feelings with the instinct of an animal. The signal now is danger and when you're alone in the woods you have to consider it. I'm hesitant, but decide to move toward Boundary Pond.

Not more than 10 minutes from my restart I cross fresh moose prints. There are splashes of water around the prints telling me the animal just left the area. I follow them to an inlet marsh and gaze into its beauty. The place is serene. Prairie grass and water combine to heighten my wonderment. This is the highest quality of "being" you can experience. It is experiencing the "now of life."

Yet even this "now of life" gets better. As I scan the inlet a female moose comes into sight. She shelters two calves. I have never seen a cow with such young calves. They are only a week or two old and follow their mother into the quagmire while peering at me with innocent curiosity. Suddenly it occurs to me that I am probably the very first human they have ever seen. They too are in the "now of life" and together we are in harmony with nature. The mother wades into deep water and the babies swim ahead and rest on some grass. I stay for a while and watch with my binoculars and then move out.

The road ahead is long and arduous. The climbs are hard at times because the ground is soft, with new gravel to replace the spring washouts. Also, there are decisions to make on direction, as I follow what appears to be the main road. Mile after mile drifts by and no pond. Each corner beckons me forward. I am getting increasingly hesitant to continue but keep going anyway. Finally, at mile 22 I stop and turn. I'm going back. It's getting really gray. I need to listen to my instincts and not be greedy. There will be another day.

The trip back is much easier as the downs overshadow the ups. Along the way, yellow and black butterflies comfort me for the distance. Sure enough, the first water drops hit my hat at mile 31. With three miles to go, I get drenched, but I'm not disheartened.

It feels good when you listen to your instincts and things turn out right. I guess this is one reason why I ride alone on a one-speed bike. It forces me to strike a balance between mind and body. Struggling physically enhances your capacity to think clearly. Try it and see.

Power of the Mountain

I'm still in Pittsburg. Still writing in a cabin on the porch. I mentally review the adventures of the past two days. They were good. Two days and I never crossed the path of another human. I traveled 75 miles—just me and my one-speed. Let me tell you about it.

The morning is clear after three days of heavy rain. The air temperature is "Canada express" (cold), the sky is cobalt blue, and the wind is in charge. I park the car off the tar on Route 3 and mosey on into the real world. Today I'm wearing my special black-pocket T-shirt with an old, black cutoff sweat shirt on top. My lucky hat and coins are with me as always, and I'm going someplace new.

The rule I follow in the wilderness is to never drive into it with a car. I save all the dirt, mud and excitement for two wheels instead of four. In this way, I preserve the newness for biking. I'm heading northeast on Smith Brook Road which starts at the northern tip of First Connecticut Lake.

The road crawls up for four miles. I decide to take a right on a gated road. Gates intrigue me. They shout at me, whisper to me, or pretty much do anything to get me in. This one's no different. I already passed one orange bar (gate) about two miles back. But two in a row I can't do. As I advance through the gate, I immediately notice the road turns soft. Snowmobile routes heave and get mushy especially when it's wet.

After a few miles of tough pedaling I break into some of the prettiest country I have ever seen. Mountains and streams surround me in all directions. Acres of trees have been taken out from old logging operations leaving beauty and vastness. I can't believe I've stumbled upon it.

In the distance I see the curling gravel road as it ascends the mountain. My goal is to get on the right track and move on up there. As I proceed I feel myself literally shrinking while the wind

Bob cats flourish in mountain terrain. Seeing one is the cat's meow.

takes full control of the day. I'm getting so small that fear is taking hold.

I fight off apprehension by refusing to put on the heavy shirt I have wrapped around my seat. In my mind if I put it on, fear will win. Instead, I struggle for reality while continuing to notch upward. There are spots where the sun is fighting for control helping me grow to size. Yet my balance and breathing are affected by the cold Canadian gusts. The wind, combined with the high-terrain angles, is taking its toll, but ironically I'm sweating.

I persevere through all the strange feelings to get to the end of the road, all the way up. The view is superb, featuring 50 miles of panoramic ridges and valleys including the large Connecticut Lakes. This is probably the best total wilderness scene I've seen in a long time, and I've biked thousands of miles in the North Country.

At the top, I find a calm spot and stop for a few minutes. There, down in the mud and water are the only creatures I've seen. Polliwogs. As I watch them dart around immune to the cold, it occurs to me that life is so diverse—and special. These polliwogs look so big in their little muck hole and I know why. It is their time to thrive on what nature has given them. If they wait, they won't survive. It gets me wondering if the wind will dry up their world. Suddenly my eyes well up as I'm reminded of how cancer came along and dried up my father's life last year. I hope the polliwogs have a better chance. All they can do is try their best to live for now, while things are right.

I'm heading down. I feel uncharacteristically weak up here in the timber today. I'll come back another time. I let my bike fly down the road. The wind tries to stop us but can't. My eyes detach and witness the whole thing as trees bend and crack along the way, yet we keep descending in spite of it. Down on lower ground my strength returns. And just before leaving, I glance back and give reverence to whatever is there.

In no time, I'm back at Smith Brook Road and heading north-east again. The road goes up for a couple more miles and then slopes in my favor. I enjoy it for awhile until another gate shows up. But I go straight deciding to turn back when the odometer hits 20 miles, and it's almost there now. The trip back is only nine miles, if I don't go off anywhere.

Well, I do go off a little so my odometer is hitting 35 when I reach the car. I'm putting the bike on the rack when it happens. I hear a screech from a truck on Route 3 and then see a little moose calf hit the dirt. The mother watches 10 feet from the road. The calf is not touched. It lurched out of the way to avoid the truck. Then it jumps up and tears off past me into the woods. The animal couldn't be more than three weeks old. Meanwhile, the mother goes berserk.

First she faces down the truck driver until he decides to move on. That leaves me standing there. Vulnerable. The cow stares at me for a long time and then enters the bushes to seek out her calf. I can't tell her but she's going the wrong way. Soon she comes back, grunting every few seconds to call her calf. In the meantime, I get the camera from the car.

The mother continues to stomp around—her back up with hair standing on end. She passes between me and the trees at least three times. I stand motionless and snap a picture when she storms by. It's important not to provoke the creature while it's distressed and I don't. Soon she leaves and I don't see her anymore. So I leave.

145

It's a Lot Like Life

Earlier today, I took my one-speed mountain bike to paradise. Come along I'll show you where I went. But first, let me explain something.

If you have been following along with me on my adventures you must be wondering why I'm still here. Well, it's simple, Pittsburg has a tremendous amount of wilderness. This is my seventh day out here and every one has been new territory. You can't beat it.

Today is one of those brisk mountain days. Puffball clouds are streaking across the sky as I ride north to park my car. I enter the woods heading for Coon Brook Bog, which is only 2.5 miles northwest of the first Connecticut Lake.

The ride grades up for almost the entire way, but not steeply. The cool wind is moving 10 or 15 miles an hour, which makes traveling quite refreshing. Soon, about two miles in, I encounter some logging operations. I decide to watch for a few minutes after I wave to say hi. Everybody waves to you in the North Country. You feel welcome, you know what I mean.

There is a man operating a machine that picks up cut logs and drops them into a truck. Another guy is walking around the tree pile with a chain saw cutting about 16 foot lengths. Still another has a sort of bulldozer that is pushing all the cut lengths into a pile. It's really fascinating to see. The mud and fresh cut evergreens combine to scent the air. I love it, but it's time to move on.

I squeeze by the loggers, trying my best not to inconvenience them in any way. Then almost immediately the road dead ends. I've missed my turn. So I go back, feeling kind of strange since I just passed by. No wonder they are looking at me and smirking. It's time to check my map.

I should have taken a left at the camp. And just beyond it, is Coon Brook Bog. Every time you break into the clear on a bike,

Beavers are the architects of the bogs. Early risers get to see 'em.

it feels like you're instantly rejuvenated, no matter how tired. I almost shiver over the feeling. This place has a spillover dam and the wind is pushing some water over. Believe me, there is something very special about these areas. They are life's sanctuaries.

I spend a long time gazing over the slightly choppy water watching the swamp grass give in to the wind. All the while the mountains peer at me. I know there is life personified out in here, but not for humans. Instead, it's nature's city.

This place was thriving eons before any people existed. We like to consider ourselves survivors, but let me tell you, this bog is a million times more versatile. Every time I visit one I can feel my sixth sense awaken, making me wonder if I've been here before. It's happened to you too, hasn't it?

Sometimes I sit in a marsh like this for hours, but today I want to see Big Brook Bog. The trip is only five or six miles from here so I return to Route 3 and head north. I'm embarrassed because I'm riding on tar but the dirt road is only a mile up on the left, and I can't get there any other way.

Farther up the way toward Big Brook Bog I have to stop for a different logging operation. This time there are two machines. One that picks up the logs and a second that saws them. This cherry picker thing grabs 50-foot trees and lifts them like nothing. Then it drops them into a flatbed, where an attached saw cuts them.

It's wicked interesting and gets me thinking. Without these operations opening up land, it would be almost impossible to see this beautiful wild country. I'm appreciative.

Big Brook Bog is about 2.5 miles from the tar and is real noisy, with animal life, but it's quiet if you see it right. Everything comes together here. It's a place where you can forget all your problems. The bog, marsh or swamp, whichever fits your fancy, is life's eternal healer of pain. Anyone who wants to fit in will feel good, and live for the moment. Try it.

From here, if I go northwest I should be able to hook up with Perry Stream, according to my map anyway. Yet, I've taken all the roads available, only to reach dead ends. Each try was a climb just like life.

I'm telling you mountain biking *is* just like life. When you try, climb and dead end in life, your reward is wisdom. When you try, climb and dead end in biking, your reward is the trip back. It's the same thing. I learn something about myself *every* day I ride. We'll talk more about it another time. Until then, ride quiet in the wilderness.

Philosophy: Mountain Bike Steve 101

No, I'm not in Pittsburg, instead I'm home wishing. I've taken you out in the woods with me a number of times. Today come along for a ride of thought.

Sometimes people get going so fast, they lose track of the important things in life. When this happens, there is an illusion that blocks out reality. And usually this illusion consists of material goods. As a result, happiness begins to slide and soon the fast track becomes a burden.

Recognizing the rat race is not always easy when you're in it. Looking left you see others moving along generally at the same pace. Looking right you see some "speeding ahead" and still more "falling off." Because you're competitive, you try at least to stay with the pack. But everyone is hurrying, so tension builds and happiness slides once again.

Trying to figure out what is happening when your life is caught up in this super highway is tough. Time becomes more important than your real priorities. Harried, you make lousy decisions, try to cover up mistakes and blame anyone and everyone you can, except yourself. Consequently, you change from your once likeable self to somebody you dislike, and happiness plunges.

The thought of "falling off" to the right creates a tremendous sense of panic. Fear is a better word. You begin to see yourself potentially as a loser in distress, and this feeling causes even more problems. Yet in your heart you know the answer but are afraid to ask the question. Instead, your life turns into a runaway train. What do you do?

Well, there are options. First, you can do nothing and hope that the train won't crash. Secondly, you can take your foot off the accelerator and "fall off." Thirdly, you can ask the question, "What things are really important to me?" If you use your instincts, you'll ask the question.

The pine marten is a cagey member of the weasel family. You won't want to get into the "fast lane" with one of these characters.

That's all it takes to gain control. Now that you have asked, you can go ahead and give the answer already waiting in your heart. Immediately your stress level drops, the pace slows and you begin to take hold of your life again. But the rat race continues, still hoping to get you back.

In order to fight off the urge to re-enter, you must ask more questions. What changes do I need to initiate? What really makes me happy? How do I begin my new life-style? Remember, all the answers are in your heart, but you must ask the questions. Then it's just a matter of being honest with yourself.

I guess you're wondering why I went through all this. The reason is simple. Most things that are important in life, are simple. Yet we live in a complex, fast-paced economy that is pushing us toward pain. By talking about it I hope to remind you that you can control your destiny by going back and asking basic questions. And at the same time you can keep abreast of the important priorities too.

For me, that's why I ride a one-speed bike. It's simple. Yes, I can afford a 21-speed. Yes, it would be easier for me to ride. Yes, it would be easier to climb. Yes, I wouldn't have to walk my bike. Yes, I would be able to speed in the woods. Yes, it would be lighter to carry. Yes, I could be like everyone else. But these affirmatives do not answer *my* important questions.

Also, the one-speed does not give me the illusion of happiness. It's real. In fact, in terms of present-day technology, my bike is like the horse and buggy. However, it makes me happy for all the right reasons. Therefore, just because the world is producing a 21-speed bike, that in itself, does not mean it will bring happiness to the rider. Quite the contrary.

In my case, I'm not looking for an easy life. Things that require little effort also generate little reward. On the other hand, to struggle through the journey relying on the simple grit in your belly brings great feelings of satisfaction. The one-speed forces me to rely on myself and not the machine. It challenges my stamina to choose the illusion of "easy life" or accept real life. I could quit and buy the so-called best bike anytime. But I don't, because most times the long, hard way around is the quickest and surest route to happiness.

Well, I think it's good to talk about these issues on occasion. Adventuring involves all of the physical and all of the mental too. Things should be balanced. When they are, you'll know. You'll be happy. I can't wait to get back in the woods again, but until then ride quiet in the wilderness.

It's a Wild Life

Today I had a fantastic run. I'm in Pittsburg, of course. It's late afternoon. I've just returned from Indian Stream. Here's what happened.

Last night I tossed and turned in anticipation of the trip. I'm up with the first birds and take a look outside my cabin. It's foggy, cold. So I wait an hour and leave at 6:30. I head down Route 3 to the first road past the Highway Department. There is an old white house for sale on the corner, and that is Indian Stream Road. I park off Route 3 and start floating north.

I've been here once, about a year ago. I still remember it because this area is truly from another world. One thing I recall is how easy going it is. After biking 255 miles in six days I need a flat ride. This is my last day in the North Country, and it's a great one.

The morning fog is lifting on the stream at the same time that the sun is beaming through—emphasizing the fantastic colors of the wildflowers. It could be Vermont, with acres of farm and pasture surrounding the meandering water as it snakes its way south. Yet, the complement of new-leaf green is New Hampshire all the way. And believe it or not, a light frost is just wearing off. It's a normal July morning in Pittsburg.

Up on the right side of the road, about four miles in, I get my first treat. I can see a bog behind some bushes and trees, so I decide to walk into the brush and take a look. Sure enough a young male moose and a young male deer are there. I pull out my binoculars and watch what goes on.

The moose is standing in belly-high water eating from the bottom of the bog. He dunks his head, gets some vegetation and comes up splashing water everywhere. He sees me but is not bothered. The deer is on the other side of the bog in knee-high water also eating vegetation. I make a noise and the deer looks at me but can't quite make things out. He keeps moving his head side to side as if to say, "What the heck is that?" Meanwhile my

Pileated woodpeckers are wild, elusive and shy, and have a
distinctive call. Look for them flitting around the streams.

view is perfect at 150 feet. Finally, the deer recognizes me and jumps away.

Moving on up the road that winds its way along the stream, I see deer number two. This time I'm only 100 feet from the deer and it doesn't run. Instead, it stays fixed without moving for a long period of time. I stay fixed too. The staring contest goes on while the flies chomp down. It's not long before I quit and move but the deer still does not take off. It stands there moving its head from side to side just as the other one did. Eventually fear sets in and the doe high-tails it. I must look strange on my bike.

This scenario occurs four times during the morning. In every case the deer are small and probably no more than three years old. When a deer "high tails it," they turn and jump away bringing their hind legs way up while "flagging" their tails. This is done to warn other deer, specifically their offspring, that danger is present. In early summer deer have a full, brown coat. They are beautiful animals with big eyes compared to their head size and it's very special to see one close enough to appreciate these features. Be patient and you'll see what I mean.

Traveling north has me bearing left to follow the stream. There are a few roads to the right which lead to Perry Stream, another paradise. Further on at 14 miles up the road a sign appears. It's the west branch of Indian Stream. I take it because I know it leads to a tranquil body of water called Terrell Pond. The gravel follows one side of the pond and beyond in a northwest direction for another few miles where it stops.

Last year I went to Terrell Pond but never followed the road to the end. Also I did not take the middle or east branch roads either. Today the real adventure starts now because its all new from here on in. When I get back to the fork where the middle branch begins, my odometer reads 21 miles. I decide to find out just how far this road goes. A trucker once told me it ends 100 yards from Canada. The map shows the road going another 3.5 miles north. Let's see.

Well, at 24.5 miles, I'm still going. Soon after, at 25 miles, I cross a bridge. If the map is right I'll see a road to my right and I do. That should connect with Perry Stream six miles from here. I'm not taking it. I want to see how much farther the middle branch goes and when I hit 27.3 it ends. If this is the closest spot to Canada, I'll go to the very end just to say I was there.

The trip back is vacation and is a little more than 20 miles. The hills are not tough on Indian Stream. In fact, they alternately climb and descend in a very pleasurable way. All along the way are scenes of giant wildflowers standing six feet tall. This is an artist's dream with colors radiating from every angle. Contrast is a key to happiness.

Indian Stream is the ultimate ecosystem. It reminds me of a jungle. I see orioles, cranes, flickers and many other kinds of birds. A highlight of the day comes when I encounter two pileated woodpeckers. They are big in comparison to southern versions and rare in New Hampshire. All I get to see is a glimpse of their prominent red crests as they cross over the road.

Soon I'm at the same bog I visited this morning four miles from the tar road. This time a female moose is in the water. She is in deep water and is thrashing around, dunking her head and seems to be having some fun in addition to eating. However, I'm not sure moose do that, you know, like elephants. But it's a new thing to see and I enjoy it for what it is.

For those of you who are not ready to bike heavy hills and mountains, Indian Stream is a good alternative. I've traveled 48 miles today and averaged 8.3 miles an hour. For me that's too fast. But it's easy riding. Normally I travel six miles an hour, not including stopping time. The slower you go the better your day will be.

Routinely Beautiful

I've just returned from a 41-mile, 8-hour trip. The Pittsburg area has so many remote miles I'll probably be here all season before I know the place. How lucky can I get? Come with me on this one and you'll agree.

The morning is one of those rare a.m.'s without fog. It's 6 o'clock and I'm heading in from a familiar spot on Magalloway Road. Today the plan is to seek out every nook and cranny that has been whispering to me as I passed by on previous trips— including a couple of gates.

The first gate appears at mile 9. Last month I suffered for a couple of miles on this road. It was wet and I felt as if I were pedaling in quicksand with my brakes on. Consequently I turned back.

Well, it's not much better now except the ground is dry. Some of these areas are open for snowmobiling only. Therefore the gravel expands with the weather, making it tough to ride in. But I'm going the distance so I can find out where it goes. Sometimes sticking to a plan is the best choice in life. You may stumble and fall a few times but in the end you're the happiest because you've seen it through.

Standing and cranking hard on flat ground is an understatement here. I glance back to see my tire tracks two inches deep. My tolerance is being tested. The only thing that is keeping me going is the beautiful mountainside ahead of me.

Then, just as I am wishing for a bike with gears, it happens. The largest cow moose I've ever seen jumps out of the bushes 10 feet in front of me. It takes place so suddenly I almost fall off my bike.

After swallowing my heart I watch the thing trounce over the road with its head and hair at attention. It careens off into the woods at maximum speed dropping everything in its path. Long

**Partridge proliferate in Pittsburg. Say that three times fast!
Whaaahooo!**

after she is out of sight I can hear her snapping branches and stomping the ground.

Don't let anyone convince you that moose are stupid or slow. Quite the contrary. They are beautiful members of the deer family and creatures of awesome power. If you ever see one scared you will witness their speed, too. Yet, with few natural predators it's not often that you see them pedal to the metal. Instead the picture you get is an animal that holds its ground or retreats reluctantly. In their own habitat they'll outsmart you any day of the week, if that's their intention. Anyway, I wait a few extra seconds to give my ticker a chance to recover, then move on.

The traveling is mostly up for two more miles and finally dead ends on the side of a mountain. The views are good. On the way back, believe it or not, the cow moose is back to her haunt.

This time we make eye contact at 200 feet. The road curls so I lose sight of her up ahead until I come out of the bend. Then she takes off again but this time stays on the route I'm taking. I continue to follow until the 800-pounder hits the forest big time, and branches die again. What a huge female.

Well, that was a perfect example of why I love gates. In fact, I'm headed toward another right now. This one is holding back the land under Magalloway fire tower. It's soft and rocky but the expanse opens up to shrink me as if I were a seedling in the company of sequoias. I'm literally below 3,600 feet of ledge. There are mountains in all directions while I wander along. I walk my bike just so I can enjoy it longer.

Soon I spot a small, dark object ahead. I sneak toward it. It's a bird. One I've never seen before. I pull out my binoculars carefully hoping it won't take flight. This thing is almost black, with some white under-feathers. It is the size of a grouse and looks like one except for one thing. The bird has berry-red eyebrows. I've seen all kinds of game birds but never one that has red eyebrows. It doesn't fly away as I creep closer. I'm so near that my binoculars won't adjust anymore. It hops onto a branch, and I notice the feet. They are brownish black with three long toes and good-sized nails. Finally I have to break away because the hen isn't going to fly off. I love to see new creatures.

Again the road dead ends and lucky for me I have to go through it all again. Actually every journey looks different on the return trip. I can't believe how much I missed the first time through. It makes you wonder how life would be if you could ride back the same way you came. I'm sure you would have another perspective. It would be interesting to enjoy but would have to be done without regrets. Riding back just to do it for the sights. Seeing things two ways is wisdom.

The adventure never ends up here even though most of the travelways do. There is no such thing as a routine. Even newness is new. It's how you look at things. I hope you saw the day as I did. Fantastic. But the road is dead-ending ahead. Until next time ride quiet in the wilderness.

A One-Timer

During the last three days I've been trying to find a route connecting Diamond Ridge Road to Stub Hill in Pittsburg. It's been wild. Ride along and experience it with me.

I head up to Stub Hill with information from the owner of Spruce Cone Cabins. He told me I could get through to Diamond Ridge if I found the connector which used to be open in the winter. He also gave me the specifics to locate Stub Hill Pond, a body of water hidden in the wilderness somewhere around 3,500 feet. The search begins.

I take Smith Brook Road to the second gate and from here it's five miles to the summit of Stub Hill. The ride periodically becomes a "push the bike" sort, as the road delves into remote and spectacular open country. In fact, only a few people living in these parts have been here in the summer. However, during the winter snowmobiles make the trek.

In any case, I'm up as far as the gravel goes, looking at my compass. The day is foggy and wet, making it impossible to see the Connecticut Lakes below. And I'm rather uncomfortable as I get ready to bushwhack into it all. The thought of getting lost up here can really spook you, especially if you dwell on it, which I won't.

My compass tips are: face the mountain, take a heading and go no further than 30 minutes. Well, at 170 degrees south, I start my climb. The terrain is steep, covered with new growth thickets, raspberry bushes, dead trees, stumps and evergreen forest. To my right are the cutoffs from past logging operations, giving me a reference point and some much-needed light. Hiking up while looking left reveals a flicker of blue in the distance. That has to be it.

Sure enough, as I move toward the water I cross an old path that brings me in. This is probably the most isolated pond in Pittsburg. Cryptic is an understatement. When, or if, you ever see

Deer can jump 25 feet like nothing. What a sight!

this place, a grin will surely appear on your face. It will be the very same look that occurred when the first human adventurer found the spot. I have the same expression now.

I've still got to find that connector. It's supposed to be in one of two places.

Descending the mountain, I take the first left and follow it to the end. It's time to bushwhack again. There is a sort-of path here but soon it occurs to me that it's just ruts from old logging areas. I trudge on and come across a fresh footprint about the size of my fist. First, I think mountain lion. There was a sighting in Clarksville or Stewartstown last week. I'm only 10 miles north. However, upon a closer inspection, I recognize the pad. It's a bear. Either way, I'm getting a strange feeling, you know what I mean. Besides, this isn't the place. I'm leaving to check out the other spot.

Here at the base of Haystack Mountain I feel confident picking up the trail. This is the area I suspected it to be. The path is heading south. That's promising. But shortly it changes into big time forest leaving me confused and frustrated. Being somewhat disheartened I bushwhack out, pick up my bike and make my way back. Along the way I think it over. Tomorrow is another day.

I talk it over with Gary from Spruce Cone and he recommends that I travel the Magalloway Road to the east branch of the Dead Diamond and then north on Ridge Road. In this way I can take the connector through to see exactly where it hooks up at Stub Hill. The search resumes.

The next morning is humid and foggy again. The good thing is that deer tend to come out from the cover when it's like this. Already I've seen three females. But what I'm looking at now is a rarity. Four bucks together in a small field and all are over 150 pounds with velvet racks. They don't take long to scatter, taking 25-foot leaps into the misty forest beyond. In another month they'll be fighting each other.

Pedaling toward my destination has me contemplating life. Yesterday I was aggravated when the search was unsuccessful. Yet, if I would have found the passage, I would have missed today's deer sightings. I've wheeled 5,000 miles in the last four years and never seen four big bucks together. Therefore, I'm locking in the moment. It could be a one-timer.

I know I'm carrying on, but it goes to show you that "failure" and "success" are just words. What counts is your outlook on things. Every second of life is new. There are no "good" or "bad" times.

After another 11 miles I am dead-ending somewhere on the backside of Haystack and Stub. From here I can see the same location where the two mountains collide, only from the opposite view. There is the trail.

This time I drag my bike because if I make it through I'll avoid about 10 miles of bike travel . Soon, dead trees litter my pathway and I find myself in muck up to my knees, not to mention raspberry bushes over my head. It's hot.

I've got to abandon my bike to save energy. The one-speed weighs a lot and I'm really having a hard time with it. I've been in here over an hour, my clothes are soaked and I'm trying to keep my cool. Panic surfaces, but I ignore it. So I concentrate on my compass and scout due north.

As I follow the heading I break the tops of bushes to mark my advance. The last thing I need is to lose my bike. Believe it or not, I break out onto gravel after a few hundred yards. It's amazing how close you can be without seeing daylight. The trick is to ignore the games your mind plays on you.

What's left is to get my bike, but when I turn, I don't recognize anything. I'm just kidding. I follow the broken twigs, get the bike and I'm free. Before I head back, I check my compass to establish landmarks. I'll never get lost in here again. It turns out the connector was over a half mile from where we thought it was. Not bad.

I learned a couple of things today. One, is snowmobilers ride on top of the jungle in a motorized vehicle. So when they tell you there's a connector, take it in stride. Two, I need to stop bush-whacking with the bike. But the truth is, if there's an adventure at hand, I'm liable to forget both lessons.

Bear-ly Moving Toward Me

Today turned out to be special for two reasons. First, I surpassed a thousand miles of mileage on my bike in Pittsburg on the trail. Second, I had my first black bear encounter.

The morning is foggy at 7:30 a.m. It's a late start for me. I park my car at the big white house on the left side of Route 3 immediately before the Pittsburg Highway Department. This is the beginning of Indian Stream. The forecast is an unusual 3H type: hazy, hot and humid. In fact, the last three days have been the same which is absurd for this late in the season. Therefore, I decide to ride Indian Stream because it is relatively easy terrain.

Most of the steep climbs are short; others are gradual and none are really taxing. However, the day will involve a lot of pedaling and extensive time on the seat which can be a burden, if you know what I mean. Yet the dirt road is hard, rather than sandy and soft or wet and muddy, so this 50-plus mile trip will have its advantages.

In my opinion, Indian Stream has the very best start and finish to a mountain bike adventure. The first mile and a half is a cozy roll through the broad stream valley with pasture land on both sides. I pass by a half dozen horses feeding on one-inch grass while all around is the one foot stuff. I've never figured out why they do that. As I cruise along, I look down to see every hair on my arms covered with morning dew.

The sun is just peeking through the fog, illuminating the thousands of intricate spider webs throughout the woods. Each micron of gossamer is covered by minute droplets of water, exposing the unmatchable construction. I can see every silk home by the side of the road. And, they're all positively unique. It's not unreal. In fact, people have the same universal quality. At times we all seem alike. Then on a special day like this one, reality shows through. We *are* different. But it's okay. It's nature's plan. My senses are primed.

167

It's not long, maybe 30 minutes, before the spectacle ends and the roadway opens up. Heading north, I skip the first left and take all the rest to dead-end more than 20 miles in. Moose prints are scarce. There are a set of tracks here but they are the only ones I've seen for the distance. This is rare. Consequently, I begin to search.

In the mud, I spot coyote or wolf tracks. Don't automatically dismiss the possibility of wolves. After all, from here I can look directly into Quebec. And let's face it, there are no fences up here. People who live here have seen them. I saw one myself last year.

The day continues to be unusual just as it started. Everything is quiet, but I don't know why. I am back at Depot Camp which is 13 miles from Route 3, and no encounters yet. I stop here and lean on my seat for a few minutes to think while looking up Ridgerunner Road.

I'm trying to decide whether I should struggle uphill to see where it goes. Finally after deciding yes, then no, I decide to go three miles. If I go farther my trip will get too long. As it is, I'll be over 50 miles for the day. I'm tired—I've already done 150 miles in three days.

The road always climbs when you're tired, but that's life. So I pump until I can't, then I push the bike. After a mile and a half, I catch a glimpse of something black in the distance. I stop and wait, peering at the shape which is now moving.

If my eyes are right, it's a bear. The animal is 100 yards away and headed toward me. The first thing I do is turn my bike around and get set to bolt. Closer and closer it straggles my way, stopping to poke around occasionally but never lifting its head.

Soon the bear gets to where I recognize that it is either a cub or a very young adolescent. Now I'm nervous. I scan 360 degrees, expecting a mother to be close by. I should leave, but I

Rumor has it that some coyotes in Pittsburg grow to the size of wolves.

hold on. I think I'll be all right because there is some open space and the mountain is behind me for a quick escape.

Beyond at 50 feet is a trickling brook. The small bruin wades into the stream and still has not noticed me. I can't believe it. Nothing happens for five minutes. I continue to survey the area and stay poised to fly down hill. The animal is less than 100 pounds. Suddenly above, an osprey lets out a screech and my heart almost explodes. Nothing else happens.

I know I'm taking a chance, but I creep toward the water. When I get within 30 feet, the bear comes out, not looking up. Finally, I have to force the issue, so I let out a snake hiss. Immediately the bear looks and veers up on two legs away from me and scoots into the bushes, leaving me with one last decision.

My instinct is urging me to turn back but I want to find out where the gravel road goes. Undecided, I do both. First I go 150 yards forward then I turn back. I've used up some luck already and I'm not getting greedy. No, the extra mile isn't worth a distressed mother's wrath. The next thing I know I'm hitting 35 mph heading back.

The rest of the trip is safe. I finish the adventure jumping a large redtail hawk feasting on a critter. What a wingspan. What a day.

A Message from the Sun

If you are stressed out from being cooped up all winter, it's time to fill your tank with energy. Come with me in a quest to link Cedar Stream in Clarksville, NH with Magalloway Mountain in Pittsburg, NH.

This trek will be new in spite of the thousands of miles I've already biked in northern New Hampshire.

In my pocket, next to my lucky silver coins, is a crude map. In my head, next to my instinct, are tips from Gary at Spruce Cone Cabins. He belongs to the snowmobile club and knows all the ins and outs of the area.

The coins are special. During WWII at Okinawa, my father received two 1921 silver dollars from his sister. She sent them dated with his birth year for good luck. He put them in his pocket and never took them out. Fifty years later in November 1992, just before he died, he handed me the coins.

They're worn smooth, but are full of meaning. Life is not a bunch of words or pictures anyway. It's feelings that count. He loved animals and wilderness but was a city guy that had some physical limitations with walking. I take the coins with me on every trip. It's my way of...well, you know.

At dawn I step outside my cabin to test the sky and air, which are blue and at 20 degrees. Motoring south for a few miles has the dew turning to ice on my windshield. I park the car across the bridge in Clarksville and head into the sun as it rises over Cedar Stream.

Traveling east in May on the very morning that leaves emerge in the forest is spectacular. While rolling along, the sun's rays flicker through the empty trees, the grandeur silently making a statement. The message awakens my spirit while my body responds with goose bumps. This day will be special. I know it.

The road stays close to Lake Francis and the going is easy. Before the odometer hits two miles, a young female moose steps out to take a quick look, then trots away. Shortly after, I notice what appears to be a brown log sticking out of the lake. But in a flash it disappears. I hang around for a second look and nothing happens. Cranking ahead I see it again. This time a good view reveals a four foot otter. Wow! It's my first sighting of otter in five years up here.

The next encounter is a deer. She sees me and is acting un-sure and keeps moving her head from side to side for a better look. Finally, I crawl forward until it flags. Another mile a thick-necked male does the same thing. Then, as I stop to tie my shoe, a large broad-winged hawk explodes from a nearby pine startling the daylights out of me. Rarely do I see this many animals within 45 minutes. But then again, a May run is unique because of open forest and spring-fevered creatures.

At mile 7 the lake ends, along with the easy pedaling. Now the gravel road twists upward. Gary told me to keep my eyes peeled for a left at the high point of the land. Well after three miles I can see things starting to level in the distance. Never expect your climbs to top off in this territory or in life for that matter. They will in their own time. All you do is keep going with grit in your belly and a grin. Don't anticipate. Instead, the rule is to take whatever comes.

Glancing out, I can't believe my eyes. There's a big black thing at 100 yards on top of the mountain. Immediately I stop and pull for my binocs. The beast is huge. It's digging and facing away so I can see the width of it's behind. It's a bear.

Suddenly, the waist belt that was resting on my seat slips, and as I reach to recover it the whole bike crashes in toward me. Fortunately I catch both while staying alert. The male bear doesn't react. He just keeps digging. Meanwhile, I put the pack together connecting it to my waist and hold my ground. He's big enough without binoculars.

Here's a wilderness-sized black bear. In Pittsburg, raspberries are plentiful. Can't you tell?

I decide to move closer since the mountain is behind for a quick getaway. Step by step I get closer. This bruin is 300 pounds plus. A spring animal of this size will be well over 400 by fall. He's a giant. When I reach 50 yards he turns, stares at me, and then goes right back to digging.

I'm wondering what the heck to do if he isn't afraid of me like he's supposed to be. I have to get by him or abort my mission. So I decide to creep forward. Ten steps later he bends, looks once, and then catapults into the ravine thrashing everything in his path. I've never seen such power. It rattles you.

Eventually I break onto familiar terrain about 20 miles from the start. Magalloway Mountain looks so majestic. I cover the remaining 25 miles back in a leisurely fashion.

In life I see it this way. If you're honest with yourself, what you think, is what you get. This mornings message from the sun translating into reality, is not luck. During the 45-mile journey my senses were enlightened with moose, deer, bear, hawk, heron, loon, squirrel, otter and various woodpeckers including a pileated. Also there were the sounds, smells, sights and most of all, the feel of a cool breeze.

A Brush With Death

I'm in Pittsburg, NH. I plan to stay a couple of nights with my friends, Gary and Dot Bedell, owners of Spruce Cone Cabins. Here, my goal is to pedal out a couple of 20- or 30- mile jaunts as preparation for the "real" trip. After a stressful year of teaching at the New Hampshire state reform school, I've set up a 10-day escape to northern Maine.

It's dawn on June 18 and I park my car outside of Baxter State Park. To drive in costs eight bucks, but biking is free. However, everyone must register with the gate warden and while I'm doing so, the warden says, "It's pretty hot to be riding today. Are you aware that it's 42 miles to the northern gate?" I said, "No, but thanks for telling me." She continued, "Do you have someone to pick you up on the other side?" I said "No, I'll go as far as I can and then turn back if I can't make it." She continues, "There are some big hills in there and the first is at mile 3." I take off without a reply knowing that it's her job to warn me, but I don't want to hear it. However, I do feel uneasy about a few things.

First is the heat. It's record breaking and humid. Second is the bugs. Bloodthirsty black flies, massive mosquitoes and horrendous horse flies are already swarming. Third is unfamiliar terrain with severe thunderstorms predicted for the afternoon. All this on top of not feeling up to par, has me tentative. Yet as I enter, I tell myself these words of wisdom: "Don't worry, make decisions."

Right now the park is like a rain forest and the sand is soft. The initial three miles has me dodging and bouncing around tractor moguls making the start a bit aggravating. Almost immediately the gravel smooths but the grade steepens and it's time to grind. The hill snakes upward for about three more miles as I drench my clothes with sweat. I'm forced to push the bike part of the way while donating blood to every species of insect. At this point I recognize that my instincts are trying to pass on a message, but it's too early in the run and I'm not listening.

I continue on with the thought that I'll take things as they come. Soon the steepness levels off but the road continues to gradually climb for the next 16 miles. I have my usual two bottles of water and a Motrin bottle full of Good & Plenty's, but no food. With food you need a lot of water to aid in digestion and after biking thousands of miles without any, I've proved it's a waste. Eventually my normal energy materializes and I consider traveling at least 30 miles one way. I figure I'll evaluate conditions then.

Before you know it I'm at mile 30 with renewed vigor and some thirst which I hold off. I check my odometer computer to speculate on a total trip scenario. It'll be at least 84 miles and it's questionable but I feel strong. The device shows that I've been averaging just over seven miles an hour. At this pace the trek would take over 12 hours. I decide to pick up the pace for the next five miles and see how it goes.

At mile 35 I feel good, dismissing the thirst. Again checking my computer for average speed I ponder the possibility of increasing it to nine miles an hour, thereby cutting trip time by three hours. Suddenly a grin appears on my face. It's the same kind that comes when someone tells me I can't do something. Whaaahooo, the challenge is on!

My spirit explodes, helping me to overcome the last hills before I reach the ranger station at mile 42. The ranger comes out to greet me and compliments my enthusiasm while I suck down a whole bottle of water. Then, I ask him to refill it which he does and tell him I should be back at the south gate by five o'clock or I'm in trouble or dead. We laugh and I'm back on the trail.

I'm on top of the world. With two bottles of water, a full container of Good & Plenty's and renewed energy, I embark on the most crucial stretch of the journey. The next 20 miles will be mostly up.

The following 10 goes pretty well. However, I use up the benefits of some candy and water, figuring the burden will be over at around mile 62. In the meantime, my recollection of the first 23

Pound for pound, the fisher cat is one of the grittiest animals in the world. If it could talk, it would say, "When it all comes down—look for me—I'll still be around!"

miles becomes somewhat clouded. This worries me because I know it means that I'm not as with it as I should be. Also another factor develops.

The sun is high, in my face and heating the ground. Land that was shaded and cool this morning is now open and radiating like a furnace. I can feel my body temperature rising while energy is being sucked from my muscles. And to make matters worse, breathing is getting difficult. This is when your two-timing friend, Panic, comes to visit.

At mile 56 I realize I'm in trouble. I can't believe just 14 miles back I had all the spunk of a kid. Twenty-eight miles to go plays on my mind like a bully in the school yard. To keep from dwelling on it, I focus on the next seven miles which will put me over the hill, (three-fourths of the way) as well as take me through the worst of the climbing...I think.

Each time I stop to drink, the bugs engulf me. During these seven miles I'm weakened considerably because I can no longer pedal up the grades that I earlier controlled with ease. I have to push my one-speed bike time and again. As I pour water into my body it floods out at twice the rate. All the while, Panic watches with a smirk. I understand what's happening, so I smile back and it becomes a game of life or death.

I shift my thoughts to a short stretch of waterfalls I saw this morning. I should be coming upon them but mile after mile passes, and nothing. Maybe I went by them while speeding down hill when sights are hard to notice. There is a stream to my right off into the woods but I cannot stop and get sidetracked. My mind is playing with me. I have not passed those falls. It's time for some candy and to think business.

There are 20 ounces of water in my bottle when I reach mile 63. With approximately 20 miles to go I plan to reward myself every five miles. Yet the odometer moves slowly in times such as these. Anyway, you need to have a strategy. That's important. I have enough candy to take three or four tablets at a time. They do not go down easily because my mouth is so dry, but they keep my blood sugar elevated and every dose rekindles some spark.

I'm getting the chills in 90 degree heat while sweating profusely. This tells me something is going wrong inside my body. But as I look down, I see my legs pedaling and that's all that counts. It's all I have, with the exception of my lucky silver coins that dad left me.

Anticipation stinks. I've convinced myself that after mile 63 it will all be down hill. What a mistake. All I really know for sure is at mile 78 I'll have a 3-mile downgrade. My senses recall the falls. They will play a role in this adventure. What role, I'm not sure. But I do know this.

Balance is the key to life. Yet, I fight to believe it as my mind teeters on the edge of mutiny. I want to stop, give up, quit, yes die but my body says it can take more. So I struggle to bring my mind equal to the task of the demands I've placed on it. However, just as I do, my body gets weak and it's my mind that keeps me going.

It's me against the odds. It's me against the nonbeliever. All my insecurities transform into people against me. They put me down, make fun of me, reject me, and otherwise do anything to see me fail. Why? Because they don't have the courage to be different, to overcome adversity, to stand alone. Instead, they choose to be negative and destructive. This provokes me. In fact, my fury triggers massive doses of adrenaline.

In this mode I take on the next hill. I make it all the way without getting off my bike. I feel like "Rocky," and tell myself that Rocky is really a story about me. Again it happens, and I explode on another hill. Victory! Yes, the falls appear.

The sight of water flowing over rocks harboring 15-20 swimmers is more than words can describe. I stagger over ripping off my waist pack and shirt, drop my half-empty bottle into the pool, and dunk my head, splashing the cool over by back. Not more than a few seconds later I'm on my knees, panting uncontrollably, with head in my arms very close to complete exhaustion. This scene continues for a couple of minutes until I muster the strength to peek above my arms. I see people staring but no one moves toward me. I stay there a couple of more minutes and resume splashing until the direct sun forces me into the trees where I sit on a boulder.

Soon my body comes back to life and I waste no time for I have 17 miles to go. The thunder rolls behind me. I push ahead. The fear of wet, soft ground also acts as motivation. Consequently, I chew up seven miles and consume my remaining water.

The way I have it figured, my trip is over when I reach mile 78. Right now I'm at 74 and losing steam quickly. I'm beginning to talk to myself again when a ranger drives by in his truck. I can't do it. I didn't struggle this long to cash in now. We wave to each other, as I rationalize that the remaining 10 miles to be more manageable than the 12 I rode in Jackman, Maine last year.

Then I had water but no candy and my blood sugar was dangerously low. Before it was over I was hallucinating. From that day on I pledged I would not go on a run without candy. Now, as random events in the universe would have it, I have candy but no water. I made it then without candy for 12 miles. I can make these next few miles and the rest will be gravy.

There I go again, anticipating. My punishment for being foolish is a very tough four miles. Occasionally a car will go by tempting me in the greatest way, to break. And fortunately no one stops to inquire because if they did, I would break. Finally at mile 78 and a half I hit the three-mile downgrade. Whaahooo! You guys got my blood this morning so if you want it now you're going to have to work for it. Come get me suckerrrrrrssss. Wheww, I needed that.

The last three miles ticked away by the yard as complete tunnel vision set in. By the time I reached the ranger station at the south gate another shift had started. I immediately asked for water. The warden started to tell me there is no water at the gate house when he stopped abruptly, looked at me, then my odometer reading of 84.45. He proceeded to reach into his lunch bag and filled my bottle with his own Gatorade. Thanks, pal. My car was only one quarter of a mile away, but I was done.

After drinking and resting a bit, I introduced myself as Mountain Bike Steve from New Hampshire. He immediately went on to say that no one has ever made the complete trip in one day with any kind of bike much less a single speed. Boy, oh boy, I'm glad I didn't give up.

The journey was long. I guess sometimes it has to be that way. Ever since my father died in 1992, my spirit left. The run on June 18, 1994 at Baxter State Park started out as just another new run for me. I had no idea the adventure would turn out to be a near-death ride. The fact that people were scattered about meant not. The search for my own identity was mine alone.

During those 84 miles I learned a lot about life. A couple of years ago, my Dad left me to go to a place I can't go. I miss him and always will. At Baxter, my spirit finally came to me with a realization. Steve, it's okay to live again.

Afterword
Point 1

In life, it's very tough to stand alone. Writing this manuscript has also been tough because it represents a "stand alone" form of mountain biking. Many publications print stories about biking adventures but few include wilderness narratives of the solitary kind. I included some of my favorites so that you can vicariously live the same excitement and awe that I experienced while "discovering" in remote territory.

I have journeyed in isolated country for a long time and only once happened upon another person doing the same thing. I was 14 miles north of Wentworth Location on the Dead Diamond River. I was returning from a failed quest to locate Magalloway Mountain and was standing over my bike, peering into a bog. As I turned to continue my trek, a man suddenly appeared in front of me and inquired about Magalloway. Stunned, I told him that it must be on the lone road I had yet to scout. We talked for a few minutes and agreed to search for the peak.

Dan and I took the only unexplored road left for nearly six miles and still did not encounter a sure sign of the mountain. It was nearly noon. I felt somewhat weary from the day's ride, and Dan was unsure about how much farther he could go, yet we edged upward until finally the tower appeared in the distance. Immediately we turned and started back because going forward would have prolonged the ride beyond our endurance.

We accomplished our goal. I felt great because it was my third attempt to find the place. So we stared back, gabbing and pedaling along the way.

I brought Dan to Mountain Bike Steve Lookout, a place I had found and named weeks earlier. There, where we had an awesome view of the surrounding mountains and a river valley below, we became friends. We took turns spouting our philosophies and in the process, conversation became open and deep. He related personal concerns about his life and I followed suit. For-some strange reason, we let go of inhibitions, and before the ranting was over, both of us had wiped our eyes at least once. Dan was unhappy with his behavior because he felt he wasn't disciplined enough about every day events, while I expressed worries about family circumstances and my health.

He reached into his saddle bag for a book and began preaching Eastern philosophies. At times he raved. I listened for hours as he passed on ideas that ultimately changed my outlook and are still helping me become a better person. In return, I passed on some wisdom of my own. We thanked each other and then prepared to leave. Two complete strangers who became good friends in one afternoon.

Near the cars we took pictures and offered encouragement to each other, and we parted. I have not seen Dan since. However, during the course of that afternoon I mentioned to him that I was thinking about writing a book of my adventures. His response was, "Don't do it Steve. These territories are domains for types like us—only. If you write, there will be hoards of bikers invading the region. And, they won't ride the right way." At the time, I agreed. I hope you prove to do it the right way.

Our encounter was years ago. In the meantime, I have been riding my heart out. During this period, I have concluded that remote mountain biking will eventually become popular for mainstream New Englanders. The network of roads already exist—snowmobiles, hunters, boaters and fishermen continue to use them as they have for decades.

I believe readers deserve a down-to-earth portrayal of remote mountain biking. I felt that I should do this rather than risk having someone else do it with less candor and forthrightness.

Point 2
Most battles are fought in the everyday arena where our spirits become swords, and our character, shields. Living really has very little to do with material things because we are all emotionally vulnerable. And we all have to choose our own paths, too.

Most logging roads are hard-riding passages which dead-end. However, this does not mean that traveling on them will bring less pleasure or reward. Yet, experts spend much of their time directing us away from these lanes just because to them they don't go anywhere—they simply end. Furthermore, experts mistakenly advise against challenge, risk or uncertainty, which causes many to lose out on an opportunity to accomplish a goal. On the other hand, adventuring nurtures instinct, elevates self-confidence and reinforces discipline. It'll transform your struggles on the outside into gains for the inside, especially when dead ends force new beginnings.

The forest will welcome you if you respect it, so go slowly, be humble, and enjoy what nature has to offer. The normal order of random events in life will continue to present hardships for us. The key is accepting adversity no matter how it strikes. Therefore, when fear comes around—smirk, when panic surfaces—think, and most importantly, when glory makes its presence known—howl. Whaahooooo!

Point 3

Throughout this book I have tried my best to present wisdom in a way that parallels biking with the human condition. However in doing so, I may have understated the pure, old-fashioned fun of it. Now, as my pen is running dry, I want to devote one last fling about the positive, exhilarating aspects of mountain bike adventuring.

Mountain biking is unique and all-encompassing. To roam the woods in all kinds of weather, in seclusion, and in glory, is bliss. There will be moments when you will just grin for no apparent reason other than you are genuinely happy. Time and again the bike will feel as if it's moving on its own. Quiet will also display its power. During each journey in uncharted terrain, the encounters with various creatures will engage your spirit.

The excitement you feel after you have struggled to an elevation that unveils views that span 50 miles, is unmatchable. It's immensely gratifying to know that later you will once again return to a place on the horizon—back where you began. This accomplishment strengthens you, while simultaneously revealing a tremendous perspective on life. Every cross road along the way represents an opportunity whereby decisions and consequences are yours alone.

Together you and one of humanity's simplest machines will traverse where few others have dared to go. Insights will feed your character. Feelings of individuality, discipline, discovery and confidence will soothe your soul. As you pedal along investigating remote wilderness corridors, it will occur to you that the most distant acres lie within your own being. These lands are where the forests of wisdom grow. Have fun exploring them.

This is what it looks like in the Dead Diamond River Valley at Mountain Bike Steve Lookout.

If you wish to correspond directly with Mountain Bike Steve, you can reach him at this address:

Mountain Bike Steve WT-1
Box 5561
Manchester, NH 03108-5561

Write to the address below for a FREE catalog of all Nicolin Fields Publishing's books. To order this book directly from the publisher, send a check or money order for $14.95 plus $3.00 postage and handling for one book, $1.00 for each additional book. Allow 30 days for delivery.

Nicolin Fields Publishing
27 Dearborn Ave.
Hampton, NH 03842

Prices subject to change without notice.